MW00328670

BRAND
PRIMACY

BRAND PRIMACY

HOW GOOGLE MADE COMPANIES THE KINGS OF CONTENT

CORY SCHMIDT

COPYRIGHT © 2022 CORY SCHMIDT

All rights reserved.

BRAND PRIMACY

How Google Made Companies the Kings of Content

ISBN   978-1-5445-3239-4   *Hardcover*

      978-1-5445-3240-0   *Paperback*

      978-1-5445-3241-7   *Ebook*

CONTENTS

INTRODUCTION

GOOGLE HAS GIVEN BRANDS THE OPPORTUNITY TO GAIN A ton of valuable traffic, but it has always amazed me to see that so many companies do not take advantage of this. Even in an industry like software that is more agile, up to date, and could benefit greatly from taking advantage of the opportunity Google has given them, they still do not. It both fascinates and shocks me to hear things like "we do not do search engine optimization" from marketing teams at software companies.

The benefits of harnessing organic search traffic are massive. For most industries, organic search is valued in the billions. I have seen companies burning a ton of cash on ads lower their cost per acquisition greatly by harnessing organic search. More importantly, with the content they create for Google's audience, they are building a great, long-term brand.

For me, search engine optimization (SEO) was a natural part of my career progression and something I was interested in since university. It is a beautiful thing when the hobby or skill you are most talented at, something you have crafted your entire life, becomes one of the most sought-after things in a growing industry. It is even more satisfying when your skill used to be "unimportant."

In the movie *Rain Man,* Tom Cruise's character was unimpressed by his brother Ray's abilities until those same abilities won him money counting cards at the casino. Some people do not value the talents of the sanitation crew in their city—that is, until they go on strike. For me, I excelled at writing—something the business world used to look down on as a potential career talent. My first venture into the SEO career path happened indirectly while attending university. Little did I know the entirety of my university studies would take center stage as the most sought-after talent in the future of algorithms.

A major change was taking place that would elevate the importance of my abilities to the top. This change involved the landscape of SEO and how it would affect brands.

I should point out that writing alone was not the key to my eventual success. It was a combination of learning the ins and outs of the SEO game and my ability to write copy that spoke to the average person. Though I began my journey with a writing background, it developed into an SEO background.

Eventually, my understanding of Google's algorithm and how it caters to brands, combined with my writing talents, allowed me to work with companies in dire need of SEO help to push them to the top of the rankings.

When I deepened my understanding of the nature of SEO and brands, I realized something was happening—something many did not realize. Brand Primacy—the concept that brands have advantages in Google rankings—was king, and I did not understand why some brands were not taking advantage.

So many brands depend on organic search traffic for sales or leads. For my industry—software—organic search accounts for roughly 40 percent of traffic. Higher in the funnel, potential customers are searching for things around a product offering. Brands that do not create content to satisfy these queries are allowing their competitors to get the first touch on prospective customers and miss out on a valuable moment in the purchasing process.

It struck me there was a serious demand for this type of information, and no one was talking about it or its effects. So, I decided to write a book all about Brand Primacy. I would like nothing better than for brands who are struggling in the SEO game to learn the ideas from this book and turn their fortunes around.

Everyone loves a success story. They especially enjoy success journeys filled with creativity, risk taking, and gaming the system. My success story stems from a background of creativity—one in which I counted cards at the metaphorical Google search ranking casino and won. And guess what? There is no mafia pit boss waiting to kick you off the Google table.

Instead, my behavior is encouraged. Google is not only bringing you free drinks to keep you playing, it's opening the vaults and letting you look around. In fact, as you will soon learn, many top brands are gaming the system of Google for their own benefit.

Some are doing it more successfully than others. That is the reality of brands and Google rankings, and there is an empty seat with your name on it. Actually, to be more accurate, there is a red carpet with your name on it. Google has rolled it out and positioned it directly in front of a set of search results.

Brand Primacy is at the center of all this, and this book will give you a detailed breakdown of what this concept is, how it is changing search for businesses, and how you can benefit.

This book generally does not focus on technical SEO issues, but the ideas and concepts you will learn are a large part of the SEO puzzle—pieces that often go overlooked.

A QUICK INTRO TO THE AUTHOR

You are probably wondering, why me? How was I able to do it? How did my background allow me to take a creative approach to reach the top of the SEO food chain? My moves were a natural reaction to the situation I was facing. After all, no one sitting at the top takes the same risks to maintain their status. Since I got my start learning about SEO for a smaller company, I had a mountain to climb.

I began my SEO career working for a software company that depended on organic search for its traffic. Like most people, I started off learning technical SEO. I was tasked with content management, and the small marketing team was focused on ranking in Google. Over the course of a few months, I realized nobody knew what they were doing in SEO. When I asked questions, they would say things like "backlinks are really important, and that is what we are trying to get" or "we need to write as much content as possible about our software and have Google index it." A lot of what I learned at the company did not align with what I read from reputable sources.

I eventually met an SEO consultant and asked him who was doing the best SEO. He said publishers who depend on Google traffic for their revenue. Upon learning this, I applied to work for publishers with big domains (lots of Google authority) and tons of Google traffic with big growth. I landed at a tech publication in Berlin with some forward-thinking SEO consultants. I learned more about SEO in a week there than I had in a year at my previous company. There were seven editorial teams, and every one of them had their own SEO consultant who advised them. They were incredibly meticulous and brilliant. They focused on content SEO, something that is now more widespread in marketing departments but at the time was cutting edge. We had massive results. One article our team wrote racked up 10 million views in a couple of years. They were making so much money on search traffic, our team alone could have financed the entire company.

After this experience, I knew what to do at my next marketing position to get search traffic. And I also knew the power of what SEO can do for a company brand. I went to a San Francisco-based digital asset management company in their Berlin offices to work in their marketing department. Their current strategy had some focus on SEO but, like most marketing departments, had more of a technical and backlink focus. I implemented the content strategy I learned and paired it with their solid tech strategy. The results were incredible. Our organic traffic went from a few thousand a month to over 100,000 a month. We ranked first for nearly all our important business terms. We converted a ton of leads from organic traffic. And, most importantly, we took the company from a small startup to exiting to a private equity company in four years.

I went from a content writer to head of marketing, leading a department of fifteen people due to my ability to harness the power of SEO.

I soon realized my SEO knowledge was like owning the only flower shop in town and the value of roses was in the millions. Furthermore, there was such a high demand for these pretty red flowers, and suppliers were so few. Now it is time for you to capitalize on this knowledge and create your own flower shop of SEO skills.

In this book, I will unleash my SEO secrets, particularly in relation to Brand Primacy. I will go into detail about how this entire setup came to be, how successful brands are using Brand Primacy to beat the competition, and how you can throw your brand's hat into the ring, so to speak.

You will learn how to move up in the Google rankings for your most valued business terms and be given concrete details and explanations of the best ways to remain competitive in the SEO world. The fact of the matter is, if you are a brand, there is an edge to be had, thanks to Brand Primacy. I am going to get you that edge.

1

BEFORE WE GET STARTED
SEO FOR BEGINNERS

I KNOW WHAT YOU ARE THINKING: *NOT YET ANOTHER BOOK, article, video, etc., trying to explain what SEO is and how it works.* First of all, this book is not an SEO manual in the slightest. I will be tackling a concept that could change marketing forever. However, a basic level of SEO knowledge is required. Now, believe me, I have met people throughout my professional career with all different levels of SEO knowledge, and what never ceases to amaze me is how little—even the ones who claim to be experts—truly understand about the subject.

If you are someone who feels they already have all the basics of SEO down, feel free to jump into Chapter 2 (though you

1

may risk falling into the above category of someone who *thinks* they know, but is overestimating his or her abilities!).

If you cannot grasp the concept of SEO, this chapter is for you. Part of my career trajectory has been paved upon helping people understand concepts that are otherwise tough to grasp. Though this book is not an SEO book per se, having a basic level of general SEO knowledge is crucial. Finally, let me assure you, I will do everything in my power to give you a fresh angle on this information, so you will be able to see things in a whole new way—a way that will help you understand and remember the concepts.

WHAT IS SEO, REALLY?

SEO is search engine optimization. So, what is being optimized here—the search engine itself? Is someone tweaking Google to work better? No, the thing that is being "optimized" in search engine optimization is the website or webpage listed in search results on the search engine. Here are some common clarifying questions to consider:

- **Does SEO refer to paid search traffic (ads)?** Nope, *only* organic (unpaid) traffic in SEO efforts.

- **What kinds of things affect SEO?** The following things will all be factors: domain (website) speed/

structure/efficiency, content/copy/links, social media, and changes in search engine algorithms.

- **Everyone needs SEO, right?** Yes, but some more than others. SEO is highly sought after in some industries that depend on search traffic, while less important in others. On top of this, all companies seeking SEO need different results from their processes.

WHAT IS THE POINT OF SEO? WHAT IS THE END GOAL?

The following is truly all you need to remember when it comes to SEO in order to keep your eyes on the prize at all times: *the entire point of SEO is to rank higher in search engines.* I do not know how often this concept is misunderstood or misconstrued among enterprise leaders who think SEO is necessary to achieve x or get them y. It is not. The entire point of SEO is to rank higher in search engines and get more relevant traffic. Period.

Let us say you have started a company that sells antivirus software. It stands to reason you would want to rank first on Google for the term "antivirus" (as well as many other related terms). To do so, you need to "optimize" your website for the search engines. Thus, SEO.

SOME NEED-TO-KNOW SEO-RELATED TERMS

The following are some basic SEO terms that I will be using throughout this book. Feel free to refer back to this page when necessary.

Domain—Domain and website are often used interchangeably. A domain—as we use it in this book—is simply the location of your website. For example, apple.com.

Rank 1—Rank 1 refers to being the first search result listed in a search engine's results for a certain term. For example, say you wrote an article about killer robots and published it. Whenever a random user searched for "killer robots" on Google, if your article appeared at the top in the first slot, your article would be considered rank 1.

Rank 0—Rank 0 refers to the time when copy from your article or page is pulled directly and placed in a box at or near the top of the search results. Not every search result will have this feature (known as featured snippet; see the term "Featured snippet").

SERP—The SERP is the search engine results page. It is essentially the entire page of results you get after searching.

Featured snippet—A featured snippet is found at the top of the SERP. It is a brief group of text pulled from one of the websites that best answers the search intent/question. The website in the featured snippet is considered rank 0.

Backlinks—Backlinks are simply links to your site from another site or resource.

Domain authority—Domain authority refers to a specific domain or website's expertise in a topic. For example, if you searched for "space travel," you would likely see NASA somewhere in the results, because they have authority in that topic.

Internal link—An internal link starts on a page and leads to another page within the same website/domain.

External link—An external link starts on a page and leads to another page outside of your website/domain.

Search intent—Search intent is the information the user is trying to find or question the user is trying to answer with their query. If I searched Google for "Apple phones," the search intent is for smartphones created by the company Apple, and the search will reflect that—instead of giving me results of Granny Smith apples carved into the shape of a cell phone, which would *not* be my search intent.

Conversion—There are different meanings to conversion, but in marketing, a conversion is typically whenever a user completes a certain step in a marketing funnel. Conversions are often tracked and measured in accordance with SEO efforts.

So, there you have it. SEO is the way in which we attempt to get our website's pages to rank higher on search engines. Simple. However, the path to accomplishing this is not so easy. Fortunately, this book is unleashing an idea that will force everyone in the industry to follow suit if they want to keep up. Let us begin.

2

BRAND PRIMACY
THE NEW SHERIFF IN TOWN

BEFORE WE CAN EXPLAIN WHY CERTAIN WEBSITES AND brands appear on the top of the rankings compared to others, we need to dig up the past.

When Google went live for the first time, search speed increased. This sounds great, but the problem was the sources of the information users received. The search was expedited, but reputable results were limited to publications and universities deemed an "accepted" source.

Essentially, Google had a partial solution—speed. It only created half of the answer that it would someday complete in whole. Sure, they sped up searches, making it easier to locate good information. However, the information was only as good as the sources creating it.

On top of this, Google was pushing their systems to deliver translated results for all different types of spoken languages. Unfortunately, traditional sources were slow content creators with outdated topic areas, especially when a subject was complex.

To complete what Google originally intended to do, it needed to retrieve results faster while making the sources of its content creation speed up their processes and write articles in a user-friendly fashion, for more current and relevant topics.

Let us take a moment to talk about Google. Not so much Google as a functional system, but Google as an idea. When we think of Google, we normally think of what it does for us. However, what about what Google, as a company and a brand, wants? For that, we look no further than their company mission, which is:

> Our company **mission** is to organize the world's information and make it universally accessible and useful. That's why Search makes it easy to discover a broad range of information from a wide variety of sources.

Of course, these days customers hold companies more accountable, and do not take their mission statements at face value. Therefore, we must dig a little deeper. We turn to Sergey Brin and Larry Page, Google's founders, and look for their intentions early on. They both have stated many times they wanted to make their product profitable. Because of this, they needed to deliver information faster. Making information universally accessible is only half helpful if it is not, as their mission statement also says, "useful." Fast is useful. Slow is questionable.

Knowing this, what did Brin and Page do? They came to rely on brands. Why did they do this? Because they wanted fast information; the way to get fast information was to favor brands willing to put that information out. There is some accountability to brands now, but ultimately, they want the available money, so they will continue to create content for Google.

Consider how websites are built today. Not only are they constructed to suit their customers and themselves, but there is another aspect to their construction. They are built specifically with Google in mind. Why is this? Google has become their go-to thing for attracting new customers for free. In my experience at each company I have worked with, analytics show that most traffic to their blog comes from Google.

3

GOOGLE'S EARLY DAYS

GOOGLE FAVORS BRANDS. RECENT GOOGLE ALGORITHM changes, which break apart underhanded SEO tactics, also put brands into the driver's seat of searches. This means technical tricks no longer work. Instead, brands that create great content to solve the search intent of Google's users succeed. This is a competitive advantage for brands, providing them an opportunity to reap the benefits of cheaper traffic and giving them an edge in branding. They can shine a spotlight on themselves in the most widely used search tool—Google.

The gradual shift in Google's algorithm began over ten years ago when developers realized their system was not optimized, and this shift continues today. The result is a system that has Google's best interest in mind.

I call this phenomenon "Brand Primacy." It means brands have an advantage over other websites in internet searches. Brand Primacy does not mean brands are handed an advantage. They must earn it in Google, and I offer a formula for doing so in the following chapters.

Brand Primacy has shifted the way we consume information. If you were to google "brand management" several years ago, you would have received informational websites that did not sell a product. In other words, they were not brands.

Search for this topic now and you will find brands selling something around the search term "brand management." Brands are exercising what Google outlines them to do to achieve Brand Primacy in their industry. Searchers usually accept the top results and do not dig to find more authoritative websites. Even if the users found *The New York Times* or *The Wall Street Journal* in the search results, they would face a paywall on both publications' websites.

This shift in information gathering has also changed Google. Not only in the way Google, as an entity, handles decisions concerning the results they serve, but also regarding the overall existence of the site and how it functions.

The implications of this shift are massive and could upend the media as we know it. To better understand this, we need to take a journey back in time to the '90s.

A BRIEF EXAMINATION OF INFOSEEK

In the early 1990s, internet searches were completely different, but not in the way you might think. When most people think of pre-Google searches, they envision sites like Yahoo and Altavista. However, the story starts earlier, with a search engine called "Infoseek."

Most people can tell you the difference between searching on Google versus sites like Yahoo, Bing, etc. It delivers better, faster, and smarter results consistently, time and time again. However, I am guessing not as many people can explain the differences between a Google search today and an Infoseek search over twenty-five years ago.

I was one of the unfortunate who relied on Infoseek when I searched the internet in the '90s. It was frustrating that such a seemingly powerful tool, pulled from so many high-quality resources, was feeding me inadequate options very slowly.

To understand the vast differences between now and then, let us briefly examine how Infoseek functioned. When someone wanted to find information online, they would search the Infoseek database. This would feed the user articles, but the results were limited. This is similar to what users experience today, but it was inadequate and slower. Also, the experience of searching on Infoseek was frustrating because it was hard to find things.

Why was it this way? Was it the lack of technology that search engines had decades ago? Yes, but that was not the only reason. Infoseek relied on major publications and university journal articles for the information they served to their users. Journal articles are slow and restrictive in who can write and publish them. Google still ran into the same problem of serving up authoritative results that were outdated or too structured in a way that was not friendly to non-experts in the field. The only difference with Google was you found the most relevant of these results much faster.

GOOGLE: ITS FOUNDERS AND EARLY DAYS

Google's founders were among the first people to think about search engines and the web in a completely different way. The fact that users knew which links went out from a website to other sites, but could not see the inverse relation, troubled the founders. As academics, they thought in terms of university publications, which put them onto the path of references, which transposed to backlinks.

Sergey Brin and Larry Page came up with Google through thinking about journal articles. They found that the articles linked to most often happened to be the most authoritative. Brin and Page then crafted an algorithm to give users better results by finding pages that were linked to the most. They outlined this in their *Stanford Journal* article "The Anatomy of a Large-Scale Hypertextual Web Search Engine," where the basis of the Google algorithm was first presented to the public.

Due to the way Google indirectly undermined publications from universities, it is interesting to see how it was intended to behave. Initially, and ironically, backlinking journal articles was its basis.

How the University Structure Improved Writers' Google Understanding

The movie *The Social Network* shows a young Mark Zuckerberg at Harvard University working on the idea that would eventually become Facebook. Interestingly, Zuckerberg was not creating something with the idea millions and millions of people worldwide would use it. Instead, he was crafting a system that would allow Harvard students to connect, see where they were, who they were with, etc. In this instance, at least initially, he acted in a way that followed a structure based on his surroundings.

Most writers come from these types of backgrounds, where the university structure is similar to the web structure. It was true for me, as I navigated the world of higher education. The things I was learning, as well as the structure of the system, would one day lead me to a greater understanding of Google.

Brand Primacy is the result of all that being turned on its head. Today on Google, endless information is instantly available. Prestigious publications and universities are no longer the most dependable sources for Google.

As a copywriter, I found my articles now had a chance to outrank the big guys. Furthermore, when I began working with brands, it became clear my writing was infinitely more valuable to the SEO world than the usual suspects. More importantly, brands are at the forefront, having upended publishers and universities. Today, if I wanted to learn about a technical term, I would more likely find an article written by a brand than by a university or other industry expert in the field. The efficacy of this is irrelevant (at least, for the sake of this book's topic: Brand Primacy).

All that matters is this is the way it is. Google has put one source to the backburner and elevated another: brands. The result is brands are now battling to present information in an easy-to-understand manner. Competing brands are doing so, meaning more information is now available on Google.

A little more than ten years after the rise and fall of Infoseek—before anyone caught on to Brand Primacy—Google was flooded with cheap tricks to serve up trash content, which was rewarded with high rankings.

This is where HubSpot comes into play, as it was a revolutionary figure, reversing this trend completely, and making it apparent to the field of competitors that there was a clear, new way of doing things.

HUBSPOT'S INFLUENTIAL ENTRANCE INTO THE SEO GAME

Chances are you have heard of HubSpot, especially if you have attended an SEO conference. Most see HubSpot as the leader of the SEO charge, and their rankings consistently back this up. For example, at the time of this publication, HubSpot has 3.2 million organic ranking keywords, and has an overall domain rank of 314 (US).

HubSpot's purpose is inbound marketing. They sell inbound marketing software, as well as other unique integrations for different systems.

However, what makes them a part of this story is how they approached the world of SEO and showed the light to other brands that it is their time, their big moment, to be on top in the digital search world.

HubSpot's helpful tools are a large part of what made them so successful, but we are most interested in how they managed to reverse the SEO trends embedded into our everyday lives (by doing content differently and better). HubSpot is credited with sparking the movement toward Brand Primacy.

They did this by forgoing the slimy tricks of low-grade sites in favor of high-quality blog posts and transparent, well-written, and consistent articles. They also expanded beyond the keywords one might expect them to write about.

By doing this, HubSpot forced Google to recognize them (and brands in general) as experts in these other areas, since this is what Google wanted their algorithm to feed to users to create a better experience.

Essentially, a user asks a question, and Google gives them someone who can answer their question. The point is not that Google is finding someone certified extensively to ensure the answer is perfect. Instead, the point is to quickly give a reasonable answer without excessive annoyances.

This led me (and other copywriters) to seek out legitimate authorities for certain topics, be it university publications or published authors and books. I would absorb this information, then write an article, blog post, etc., about the information in my own words, with my own style, and, most importantly, as a brand representative.

The result was my articles outranked the very experts from whom I had learned the basics of the topic. From Google's perspective, my information was much easier to digest for the average person; it was more topical, and thus, they ranked my article higher. Where traditional sources found no incentive, brands found plenty, which pushed Google to promote Brand Primacy to further incentivize brands.

To learn from HubSpot, it is important to know them and see what they did that worked. Think back to when I relayed data about HubSpot (3.2 million organic ranking keywords and 314 domain rank in the US). Similar to my personal success stories with SEO, HubSpot was created on the foundation of contrarianism. Its founders examined the status quo of Google rankings and SEO and figured out a way to go against the flow. They did this by disregarding the tactics others were using to manipulate SEO, and instead wrote good content Google felt comfortable feeding customers. Now, their impact on inbound marketing cannot be overstated.

Now let us examine why HubSpot is at the forefront of every SEO discussion.

What HubSpot Does Right

HubSpot is one of the first companies willing to favor audience-serving content over cheap, algorithm-manipulating material. They consistently create well-written articles and provide users with good information in an engaging, easy-to-read format. For example, their articles give detailed, thorough explanations about topics instead of using every post they create to sell something.

The result is a large domain that ranks overwhelmingly well for numerous keywords. They have built an SEO empire, using their blog to tackle the topics they wished to rank for, all while creating well-written pieces that serve the audience in ways other content does not.

Of course, copying HubSpot will not bring brands anywhere near the same levels of success in the SEO world. HubSpot has created such a large domain and so firmly planted themselves within Google's rankings that doing what they do will not deliver equal results. However, brands can use common principles to emulate their success. Do not neglect the foundations—a comprehensive approach to good content—HubSpot laid out as a company. They are at the top for a reason, and that has to be respected.

How Brands Can Learn from HubSpot

How can brands improve upon their structure and strategy? Is HubSpot handling SEO optimally? Are they aware of and striving for Brand Primacy as best they can? Despite HubSpot's success, they are still not putting themselves in the best possible position to use Brand Primacy and capture SEO. These oversights, which include banking on past successes and overvaluing the status quo, are a chance for other brands to create leverage—the same way HubSpot did when they entered the SEO realm. It is not a certainty, but SEO experts, including myself, have seen brands making serious waves in the rankings.

HubSpot is far from complacent in their SEO efforts, but they are also not moving at 100 mph the way they used to. Their blog posts are outsourced and jammed into a method that has proven to work for Google's algorithm. Though their content is still better than that produced by the algorithm-exploitation methods they overcame, it still has weaknesses. Is their methodology proven to be successful? Yes. Can it be improved upon? Of course.

How Brands Can Improve Upon HubSpot's Success

Brands should see themselves the same way HubSpot evaluated themselves upon their inception: they examined the market and realized they could do it better. Now, other brands are doing the same evaluations and rank-climbing.

Only, they are targeting HubSpot's claim to the SEO throne. We are seeing a lot of brands put serious effort into creating content for Google the way HubSpot did, structuring it with rankings in mind.

4

GOOGLE'S PART IN THE BRAND PRIMACY EQUATION

IT IS A CLICHÉ TO SAY WE ARE SEARCHING FOR TRUTH, BUT that is often the case. Famously, Tom Cruise demanded the truth from Jack Nicholson's character in *A Few Good Men*, only to be told he could not handle the truth. Fortunately, the gatekeeper to truth in real life is not a military officer covering up hazing.

Throughout most of this book, you will find strategies designed to help brands stay at the top of Google's rankings, reinforcing their position as trustworthy by default.

When something is in question, people search Google to settle it. Even voice-activated artificial intelligence (AI) searches pull their answers from Google. It is no surprise

Google is the arbiter of truth. "Google it" is what you do if you want to determine whether something is true.

How do you know if a brand is real? You google the brand. How do you know this brand does what it is supposed to? Google what it does. It has become the definitive way to ascertain the truth. Even when a set of results disappoints, the user changes search parameters to adjust, rather than searching somewhere besides Google.

Users know Google is their best chance at finding the real answer on any topic.

Here is something to consider: if publishers pull up as the top result in Google, they are the arbiters of truth. This is true by way of the transitive property. If Google = truth, and Google ranks a publisher highest in a search, then the publisher = truth.

However, by pushing brands up in the general rankings, Google remains the arbiter of truth because brands are not immediately trusted as news sources. Therefore, they are only trusted because Google says so. It stands to reason then, if a brand wants to be "correct," they do not need to be accurate or truthful. Instead, they need to meet Google's standards for ranking on search results.

This deserves deeper explanation. A brand with deceptive ideas will fall out of favor in the rankings, as inaccuracies are looked down upon. However, there are notable times when a brand creates an article that is elevated to the top of Google despite having bad information.

For example, let us say Apple creates a blog post titled "Top Five New Smartphones in 2021." The first four phones they list are valid. However, the fifth phone, something called the Ironplex 5000, does not exist. Despite this inaccuracy, their article would still outrank smaller bloggers on the same topic, simply because they are Apple, and Brand Primacy is in full effect.

In an attempt to build domain authority to win in general searches as well as branded searches, brands have made themselves more reliable sources of information by following Google's (unspoken, often nebulous) guidelines. This point needs reiteration because it is the key to this entire concept: brands have become reliable sources of information by following Google's guidelines and giving Google's users reliable information.

The result is a bunch of brands with an advantage over other websites producing high-quality content tailored to search audiences. Brand voices are now amplified and given more responsibility to create helpful content.

Google is the one deciding which brand's content better serves the search parameters. These actions simply give more authority to certain voices.

So then, how can brands continue to be the voice of truth? It begins and ends with building domain authority.

By building domain authority, brands enrich Google by providing their users with more accurate, helpful content. If a brand stops building the right type of content for Google's audience, Google de-ranks them on general and branded searches, creating a loss in revenue.

THE GOOGLE FORMULA

Brands must follow the Google formula if they want a chance to stay relevant. The only option is to play Google's game.

Remember, Google wants to serve brands to their users. Google and brands have the exact same goal: to help each other reach target audiences.

As domain authority boosts a brand's standing on Google, it receives more benefits. The process is cyclical and keeps the two (brands and Google) working to serve one another—

brands try to win Google's favor while Google tries to keep brands from giving its users poor content.

Organic search has become the middleman between marketing and leads. Google has a self-interest in seeing brands compete in its search engine. More search traffic to companies and more conversions from Google equals more investment in Google Ads products.

Companies think, *Most of our traffic comes from Google, therefore we need to invest more in Google.* This is true even for other campaigns like a podcast appearance. The brand is mentioned, the audience is convinced; they search for the brand and make a conversion on Google. SFDC (Salesforce) says Google is the source of campaigns, which means more money goes into Google in ad buys.

Remember when advertisements repeated the web address to ensure the audience remembered it? We would hear things like *"Visit www dot brand name dot com"* a few times throughout commercials. Instead, brands now count on Google to serve their brand to anyone searching for it in the results.

Even if someone is unfamiliar with the full name of a brand they heard advertised, they find it using Google search. As such, no one goes directly to websites anymore when discovering brands. They use Google for that.

Meet the New Boss, Same as the Old Boss

Remember how the SEO community frowned upon those who "hacked" the Google algorithm and were punished by Google's changes? As they say, nothing really ever changes. Many SEOs say they are not hacking the Google algorithm, but instead are simply providing the best experiences for users.

Unfortunately, that is not the case. They are, in fact, just as guilty of hacking the algorithm. They are doing it in a way deemed more acceptable in the modern era.

SEOs believe they are not hacking the algorithm because their interests are aligned with Google's. Their current process involves building content marketing.

This so happens to serve both direct visitors and Google visitors. However, when it comes to the Google visitor, Brand Primacy is the reason it is helpful. Taking advantage of Brand Primacy is, in fact, hacking the Google algorithm.

Let us face it—if the algorithm rewarded keyword stuffing and backlink buying, SEOs would start doing it.

Your Big Chance; Your Google Mission

Search users on Google expect the first result will be the brand they are looking for. As such, do not let them down—strive to be that first result by working with Google.

As a result of the backlink-backed algorithm, the longer Google props up brands, the stronger they become.

When looking at the entirety of this process, there are a few key things to note. One of the most important is the compounding, reinforcing factors in play. For example, if a brand can win the favor of Google's algorithm, this will galvanize their position even further—similar to the "rich get richer" sentiment.

5

THE BRAND INCLINATION ACCORDING TO GOOGLE

IN THE EARLY 2000S, A SEARCH FOR "MITTENS" WOULD have fed you results from websites that were not brands. These sites ranged from someone's ad-heavy blog about what kind of mittens they wear in the winter, to a story about someone's hilarious cat named Mittens.

The underlying factor is these are not brands. Plus, they do not feed the user the intended result most of the time. Today, a Google search for mittens gives users local options to buy mittens, as well as reputable e-commerce sites like Amazon. The latter is much more favorable. A change was needed, and fortunately for the user's sake, a change was coming.

Google wants to send audiences directly to a brand website so they can make a purchase. Why does Google want to do this? Because it is a great user experience for searchers, and a great experience from their customers means more success. Brands are now given an advantage over publications.

When I mention "quality" brands in this section, I mean brands operating within legal boundaries and not trying to trick search users into going somewhere or buying something they do not want.

Let us journey back to around 2010. Brands did not require Google for validation or traffic. That is not to say they did not need Google—they did—but the way they interacted with Google was far different from the way they do today. Brands were not necessarily listed directly on Google's SERPs. Instead, they would require a second interaction with another website.

The problem at that time, at least for a lot of legitimate brands with authoritative content and quality products, was Google's algorithm did not favor them. If you googled "insurance" in 2010, you would see ten pages of different insurance providers.

If you were an insurer, like Farmers, Allstate, or State Farm, the only way for you to show up on the first page of Google was to show up in one of those listicles or other forms of Google with their own search bar and algorithm.

Flimsy sites had found a way to stay atop the attention-drawing Google rankings through the use of SEO practices that proposed they were authoritative and deserved recognition. Mind you, SEO in 2010 was not the same as it is now. Many of these sites were not creating good content to elevate their rankings, which would be required today.

Instead, they were gaming the system and forcing brands to pay to get onto the first page of Google. Spam, as it pertained to Google at one point, meant delivering the wrong results to their users.

This resulted from keyword-jamming practices, something Brand Primacy cured. Keyword jamming was essentially getting as many of the necessary or important keywords into a post or website to make it seem like they were meeting a specific search result.

However, it was not intentional manipulations holding Google search results back. There were things such as simple errors in the way Google's algorithm worked that needed the cure (Brand Primacy) just as badly.

Of course, not everything that interrupted or detracted from the user experience was exploited or exploitable. Plenty of naturally occurring instances showed why a better solution was needed. Something that constantly reminded Google how the system was flawed was keywords.

Anyone involved with building or writing for a website is aware of the many keywords involved surrounding potential ads and content.

These keywords are much more complex when considered alongside the Google algorithm today than they previously were. In the past, a Google search for "Apple" may have retrieved a top result of a brand called *Apple Palace Apples* instead of the popular *Apple* (iPod, iPhone, etc.).

This is because the algorithm was a weak "thinker" in the sense it recognized the importance of keywords, but rewarded sites simply for repeating the keyword. The overall effect this had on the user was less time online and more frustration. At first, Google did not recognize the user frustration would cost them more money in the long run, so it took them a while to adapt.

This example seems absurd and unlikely, but there were actual times when similar things happened, like a popular college being outranked by a tiny college simply because the smaller college had numerous keywords in its name. This ended up being another correction, in a long line of corrections, sparked by the idea of putting brands forward in Google.

SEO for insurance companies and other brands then became engaged with websites like ehealthinsurance.com and other conglomerate websites. Not all of these websites are created equally—the playing field was a bit misshapen in favor of bigger domains. And usually what it meant to get into these results was a combination of review gathering and, most importantly, payment to these websites in either a bid or a subscription fee for listing.

This may sound all well and fine for webmasters—you have found a way to take your low-grade website and shoot it to the top of Google and make money from brands. In terms of fairness, as long as you are not breaking any rules, this seems reasonable. However, consider it from a user perspective.

When searching in Google for insurance, you wanted results of the top insurers for your personal preferences, based on price, location, ratings, etc. Instead, you were often fed spammy websites with rigged rankings that only led you to sponsored insurance sites.

From Google's perspective (as a company, rather than the algorithm we were previously referring to), this was not what they wanted at all. It was clear this experience was not serving their users optimally, which is the equivalent of a business upsetting its own customers.

Because most search results for brands took place inside websites other than Google, it became a middleman. Here is an example to demonstrate the way this setup operated. Imagine for a moment you have a fire in your house.

You dial the fire department, but are connected to a business called "Firezone," which passes calls on to the fire department after advertisements from sponsors. This was how Google search was operating, delivering a third-party site before you could find the service needed.

Brands had plenty to offer, but their visibility was hampered by an algorithm that was not pushing quality brands (brands committed to customer service and not scamming users) to the top. It was as if the brand had a legitimate solution to a customer problem, but the customer could not find them without going through ad-heavy nonsense. By the time they found what they were looking for, their house might have already burnt to the ground, so to speak.

The Google team realized this structure was not working for the user experience. They knew the only way their search results would deliver quality solutions would be if quality brands were favored. This would take a consolidation of terms, funneling normal words into results matching big, trustworthy brand names.

VINCE: THE GOOGLE UPDATE THAT CHANGED EVERYTHING

Anyone who has ever watched the inspiring true film *Stand and Deliver* likely has been both happy for the students of the story and simultaneously appalled by the treatment they face. Not only do they defy all odds by succeeding in a difficult form of mathematics, but they also overcome something no one likes to deal with: rule changes. In the film, the students pass their exam, only to be forced to take the exam over in a more secure location with testers hounding them the entire time. This is an example of completely unfair rule changes for sure, but in real life, rule changes—fair or not—have a massive impact on the participants.

Google's developers make changes to their search algorithm all the time to improve efficiency. There are so many variables involved in searches, and new things are searched for every day, so the algorithm has to keep up. The entire point is to evaluate the user experience through a system that favors trustworthy quality content and brands that are fair to customers and write content to actually answer the search intent.

Even though Google delivers new updates every day, these are not notable. However, they also periodically have a big update, which they assign a name to. You may have even heard one or two of their (in)famous update names: *Rank-Brain, Panda,* or *Payday.* Each one had its own specific purpose.

The major update that favored brands over publishers was *Vince.* Remember the "mittens" example, and how a search for the term would now feed you trustworthy brands? That was a result of the Google algorithm update *Vince.*

In "Google's Vince Update: The Day Big Brands Won" (*Search Engine Journal*), Josh McCoy explained, "Simply put, the *Vince* update was a quick, noticeable change in broad-level, competitive keyword terms to favor first-page rankings for big brand domains vs. previously ranking sites."

When *Vince* went live, brands started moving up the Google rankings, taking the place of the sites that were latched onto keywords like leeches. This made branded and generic searches fetch brand domains instead of other sites that only *referred* to brands. Without *Vince*, ranking as the first brand could still put you on the second or third page, behind all the spammy sites taking up the first page.

And ranking for your own brand with a branded search could leave you a few off the first page of Google as well. A quick example to demonstrate the absurdity of this concept would be if a search for "Apple" showed apple.com all the way on the fourth page of search results.

Google saw brands as a way to slice through the nonsense and give searchers what they wanted.

As former Google CEO Eric Schmidt explained, "Brands are the solution, not the problem." He went on to say, "Brands are how you sort out the cesspool."[1] Aligning with that assessment, Google changed their algorithm with the *Vince* update in 2009 and never looked back.

In the first chapter of this book, we covered the SERP feature and its importance to brands. It too was deeply affected by the major algorithm updates Google implemented. The *Panda* and *Penguin* updates specifically changed the SERP.

As we discussed in our introduction of Brand Primacy, the SERP is crucial for brands. Part of why SERP features are important is they help give information to users in the search results, cutting through nonsense and helping them find the answers and brands they want.

---

1 Meghan Keane, "Google CEO Calls Internet a Cesspool, Thinks Brands Are the Solution," *Wired*, October 8, 2008, https://www.wired.com/2008/10/ google-ceo-call.

Today's Google SERP features are much more comprehensive, allowing users to find information without necessarily even leaving the search parameters. Again, we go back to Google's main focus we have mentioned throughout this entire chapter: user experience. If someone searches Google for a specific brand, like Microsoft, they will receive three things:

1. The right site. For example, searching for "Microsoft" results in Microsoft.com as the top result.

2. A less cluttered SERP with comprehensive site links.

3. News and information about the company, sometimes from social media platforms.

And remember, this all happens inside the Google search results. One could argue it may discourage someone from clicking on the brand website, but there is some nuance to that theory.

For example, if I wanted the price of an Apple product and I found it instantly in the search result, I would not have to visit Apple's site. However, I can still circle back later (to purchase) if I am doing price comparisons first. I am also receiving potentially vital information about a brand immediately in the results, which could help serve the brand.

The landscape of web searches looks much different today thanks to Google's insistence that brands were the key to fixing it. Google decided the user was numero uno, and in doing so, delivered their customers (users) the goods.

This gives brands a distinct opportunity because Google favors brand websites over publications or ratings websites in their SERPs. As a result, brands can interact with potential customers far more quickly than ever in the search engine. The question is how to rank above other brands.

6

SERPS AND THE REAL ESTATE OF SEARCH

PICTURE THIS: A YOUNG MAN IN A SMALL TOWN SEES AN opportunity to hang his advertisements on local business windows. He notices the local grocery store has different flyer advertisements hanging up, so he walks in and asks to speak to the manager, telling him of his plan. He says he wants to advertise his lemonade stand on the grocery store's window. The manager agrees but tells the young man he can only leave the flyer up for one day. The young man goes back home, gets his flyer and some tape, brings it back to the store, and hangs it up. Later, the manager walks by the window and sees something odd. The new flyer is seven feet wide and fills the entire window, leaving no space for other advertisements.

The search engine results pages (SERPs) offer a similar advantage, though without the deceptive nature of a giant flyer blocking out an entire window.

Imagine a brand does not show up on the first page of Google. This fails to take advantage of the SERP space and diminishes credibility of the brand. In my experience, this happens relatively often because some brands are aware of Brand Primacy and the power of the SERP, and some are not.

Before we go into the breakdown of the SERP, let us give some background on brands, their prevalence in the search engines, and how users will come upon these brands.

In my industry alone, Software as a Solution (SaaS), there are thousands of companies worldwide, all with their own distinct brand. And there are millions of companies across different industries; each of them wants to have their own brand identity.

Most brands are discovered when a potential customer needs a solution. Let us say your team needs a new project management tool. You ask around and look at lists online to come up with a few to research. But let us say you remember one brand you used a few years back, Trello. How do you verify Trello is the actual brand you are looking for? If you are like most people, you google it.

The first interaction an audience has with SaaS-based and other brands (outside of China or Russia) is likely in Google, whether in a general search for something like project management or for a project management brand like Trello.

Let us look at "project management" as a search term. The average cost per click (CPC) for a bid on project management software in the United States is thirty dollars. There are 16,000 searches performed for this term in the United States every month. Achieving the top of the first page for this term would have a value of about $90,000 a month.

The reality of the current situation is every brand should get primacy. The deck is stacked in the favor of brands, and they are realizing it and taking full advantage. For example, imagine someone searches "brand management tool". The likeliest search intent is for a brand management system. Therefore, websites that offer these systems are in a great position to achieve Brand Primacy.

On top of being favored to achieve primacy, once achieved, the rewards are sweeter than they have been in the past. Google makes the SERP much more top-heavy, as we discussed earlier, making it more important to gain Brand Primacy to reap these rewards (more space, less competition, etc.).

Lastly, consider the modern Google search's inclusion of paid ads. Though this may change in the future, the size of paid ads in the SERP are bigger than ever.

In the past few years, Google increased the total allotment of paid ads, allowing four paid results at the top of the SERP. Consider the leverage of being the first organic search result as a brand. Already, almost half the page is gone to paid ads. On top of this, Google has increased the sizing of these paid ads, making Brand Primacy as important as ever.

THE POWER OF CONNECTING BRANDS TO GENERAL SEARCH TERMS

In California in the mid-1970s, someone created a brand that forced the word "apple" to be associated with both a fruit and a popular technology company. When Brand Primacy kicked into high gear, apple became associated mostly with the tech company—and the search results backed that up.

Now that we have a basic understanding of Brand Primacy (which we will be revisiting constantly throughout this book), let us discuss the importance of connecting brands to general search terms in Google.

Let us say someone searched for "brand management" instead of "brand management tool". Though both are broad searches, the former is broader. The most likely scenario is Google believes the search intent is to learn about brand management, and it feeds straightforward results on the SERP. This usually includes dictionary definitions or Wikipedia entries. It would appear brands have to take a back seat in this case, but once again, remember— brands are favored.

Using the above "brand management tool" example, how could brands make this happen?

We need to first think of how the SERP displays results to this search. If the algorithm assumes the user's intent is to receive an answer to their question, "What is brand management?" (though they did not search that directly), then it would make sense for brands to answer this question.

How do brands do this, thus increasing their chances to rank for general search terms? When building out brand management content, they not only create easy-to-read, exciting material, but also answer the question "What is brand management?" as clearly as possible. That way, they have a higher chance of becoming featured on the SERP by Google. If you are building a brand's search rankings, follow this method of creating exciting material in a similar fashion.

HubSpot, for example, is an industry leader for inbound marketing. When you consider their SERP feature, it is distinguishable as elite. It is like a magazine, with different sections to turn to (click on) that guide you where to go. HubSpot has ranked for important general terms by creating helpful content around these related search terms.

Another example to shed some light on this idea is retail. Imagine a general search for "tennis". A tennis or sports brand would strive to have their website appear close to the top, above explanations of the game of tennis. The brand would also have to compete with news stories about tennis, sites that feed sports scores, and results of major matches.

Ultimately, the SERP is going to feed users things that Google feels fit their search intent, and the user behavior of their audience will dictate this in the long run. Because Google favors brands, if companies focus their efforts on ranking for general search terms, there is a good chance they will be at the top of the page.

With that, we move to the next topic: building Brand Primacy.

7

IMPLEMENTING THE PRINCIPLES OF BRAND PRIMACY

IF YOU HAVE BEEN SWEPT UP IN THE CHESS CRAZE—courtesy of the stay-at-home nature of COVID-19 coupled with the TV show *The Queen's Gambit*—then you are likely to have heard of Magnus Carlsen, the world champion chess player. People often attempt to dissect his brilliance, and how it came to be. They look for insight into Magnus's mind, trying to figure out how he does what he does on the chessboard.

However, if someone were to take a closer look, they would be disappointed with the real answer. For all the brilliance we attribute to the chess champion, the real power of his greatness comes in the fact he worked hard. All day, every day, he played and practiced chess for nearly his entire life.

Boring, mundane practice created the illusion of genius. Now, certainly he had a brain capable of calculation, understanding, and strategy—but this was just the foundation.

Brand Primacy is similar to the creation of a world champion chess player. Even though brands have an advantage, they do not become truly privileged until they put in the hard work and build Brand Primacy.

As I mentioned earlier, I was on the ground floor when the Brand Primacy goldrush opened up, allowing me to experience firsthand how powerful brands became in Google. However, some things still hold brands back, such as matching what Google wants and doing it better than your competitors. This chapter will help you understand Brand Primacy on a deeper level and start moving you in the right direction to capture its power on your own.

Google's algorithmic advocacy of brands in its SERPs is a direction the company is pursuing vigorously, and not a flash in the pan. Investments today into brand relevancy in Google searches will pay off for decades, making this type of branding activity crucial. As you have read about throughout this book (and will continue to hear about in later chapters), Google does not favor brands by accident.

In other words, a Google engineer will not wake up tomorrow and realize there has been a mistake in the algorithm.

He or she will not be rushing to "fix" this. This is a task Google is committed to, and this task continues to be backed up and reinforced. This is why the idea of investing in brand relevancy has such a huge potential for growth.

A DEEPER ANALYSIS OF HOW BRANDS HAVE THE ADVANTAGE IN GOOGLE

The reality is brands have an unfair advantage in Google, and many are now using that advantage. We could spend an entire book talking about this dynamic of unfairness and advantages, as well as dip into how it ties into or detracts from Google's previous slogan, "Don't be evil." However, our time is better served working to succeed using the cards we have been dealt.

The competitors are subject to whatever is prevalent at the time, and for brands, Google's algorithm is stacked in their favor. What needs to be considered is how a brand can adhere to these rules and realities. The purpose is not to uncover unfairness, but to adapt to it so our competitors are not the only ones benefiting.

This advantage extends to high-value general traffic that drives leads and purchases while promoting brands to the right audience. Companies who have leveraged this in the last ten years have seen incredible success.

One such company, which we have talked about plenty so far, is HubSpot, a $1 billion–a-year (and growing) startup in marketing automation. Their biggest marketing advantage is leveraging Google to boost their lead generation operation.

This has also narrowed the places where brands can be validated. Before, you could check the legitimacy of brands in multiple websites. Now, Google is the single source of truth, where a brand can be directly linked—if they play their cards right.

Resistance to Change Is Inevitable and Normal

It is easy to point just about anywhere throughout history and show the troubles people have adapting to change. Changes in search engines and Brand Primacy will meet resistance from those who do things differently.

What will happen as a result of this resistance? First, some brands will get caught up in the past, overvaluing what has brought them success so far, and undervaluing the new ways to drive success.

As I mentioned earlier, the analytics tool Google offers shows much of a company's organic traffic is coming from articles on their website's blog. It would then be logical for brands to use blog articles to drive more traffic to themselves, right? Not exactly. In fact, many brands are lagging far behind in this area, either oblivious or intentionally opposed to the idea. The result is this: some brands thrive where others falter.

With Brand Primacy and the current Google situation, the problem arises with brands that are unwilling to admit Google is the most important part of their branding efforts. The fact is, Google "owns" part of your brand in a way, which can be tough to accept.

Here is an example: think about a company blog. For the longest time, a company blog may have been a way for a brand to express themselves to people who visited their site. However, now the blog is a way to bring people from Google to the site. So, instead of tailoring their messaging, tone, etc., for people on their site, they now tailor it for Google.

You must be willing to embrace changes to take advantage of this. By doing so, you will not only adhere to what the users want, but you will also jump ahead of the competition who refused to adapt.

This is what most brands are doing now. They realize Brand Primacy—through Google—is the way. This brings about a massive shift in their branding and marketing.

A RUNDOWN OF INTERNAL LINKS
(HOW IT ALL WORKS)

It is likely you already know the difference between an internal and external link (internal links to another page on your domain and external links to a page outside of your domain). Let us turn our attention to internal links, and how sites are using them to build better domain authority.

Companies use internal links to move their users from one page to the next, typically to get them to more pertinent information, or to move them to another page that builds off the information they are currently reading. Linking practices also affect things like SEO, so it is necessary to be effective in these processes.

There are two main things to focus on when structuring your domain's internal links: the paths the links route users through and the anchors. Let us discuss these two different key factors in further detail.

Internal Link Routing

When routed correctly, internal links send users to the most helpful information. In order to place the correct internal links, consider the type of things that would logically follow the user path. If a user searched for something and landed on one of your pages, there is a good chance it can be linked to a related page. These types of decisions will guide the linking process.

For example, if you have an article about deserts, it might be helpful to the reader if you link to an article about cactuses. Taking it a step further, you might also link to articles about hot temperatures, sand, and temperate preparation. Once these linking networks begin expanding, you can refocus on making them connect in the way that gives authority to the main article on this topic. We will discuss topic authority briefly, but first we will touch on anchors.

The Anchors

If you named a cookie business "Soups 4 Sale," it would be confusing. A similar concept applies to anchor text.

The link anchor is the text that is hyperlinked to the next page. For example, a common phrase used to link out is the word "here," as in, "check out this new information here." This idea is nothing new, by the way. In fact, Sergey Brin and Larry Page had this in mind as far back as 1995, when they built the PageRank system with the idea of making a search engine that would rank links based on how often they were being linked to.

Ultimately, anchors are important because they change the way Google understands your overarching linking system. We will discuss this in further detail in the next section.

Topic Authority

Brand Primacy encourages brands to shape their website and content structures a specific way, especially when it comes to site building and link building. This brings us to topic authority, and how brands give authority to pages they want to convert.

When you think of authority, it is hard to escape images of people in charge. It might be a teacher or police officer, but it is usually someone who has a say over you. You would likely go to them to ask permission or advice. Topic authority is like your domain's version of a person in charge. Let us make sure you can grasp and benefit from this important part of building Brand Primacy.

There are bound to be topics in your content-building efforts that are more important to your brand than others. Competing brands in similar industries are the most likely to rank for them. As such, in order to achieve Brand Primacy, brands are giving authority to specific topics within their linking structure.

For example, a brand that wants to rank for things related to mechanical pencils will create a page with the hyperlink "mechanical-pencils" and any mention of mechanical pencils in further articles will link to that main page. This is where we circle back to our internal link routing and anchors. The brand's internal link structures on their domain are built, in this case, to link to and from their main page about mechanical pencils. They would use the anchors related to these pages and whatever subtopics branch out from it. These processes are how brands achieve primacy through effective topic authority practices.

Let us take a deeper dive into how domain authority is crucial to Brand Primacy. The topical domain authority brands receive from Google is central to achieving Brand Primacy. As authority increases, brands rank better for their core terms. This in turn allows them to rank for surrounding keywords. By ranking for these ancillary terms, it bolsters their position with the main keywords. As a result, it becomes easier for brands to rank in the future. Additionally, the brand itself becomes aligned with general search terms in the Google Knowledge Graph.

If you are unfamiliar with the Google Knowledge Graph, do not worry, it is pretty easy to understand how it works. Think of it as Google's way to understand everything in existence users might search for or ask, such as "How deep can a submarine dive?" or "oatmeal cookies." This is a dynamic database, which grows and changes according to evolution of searches and people in general.

If you have seen the TV show *The Simpsons,* you have probably heard the phrase "D'oh," said by the main character, Homer. Before search engines, dictionaries were our version of the Knowledge Graph. Due to the popularity and widespread referencing of *The Simpsons,* the word "D'oh" was added to dictionaries. So how does this tie in with Brand Primacy? Imagine your brand is a word that does not exist, and it is being added to the dictionary. Pretty big deal, right? If you can navigate topical domain authority correctly, you will achieve this. Your brand gets an ironclad tie to general search terms. And once this happens, it is like having super-powers (or in this case, "Simpsonspowers").

CONVERTING WITH CONTENT

One of the new ways of doing things in the age of Brand Primacy is converting with content. You achieve this by creating content that builds out deeper than previously thought possible. Let us consider the keyword structure of many top brands. When brands are creating original content to rank on Google, they know in order to perform well on their most important keywords, they need to branch out. This is where long-tail keywords come in.

Long-tail keywords are commonly confused to mean keywords that are longer in actual length, but that is not the case. Instead, it refers to a mathematical model of x- and y-axes containing searches made for different keywords. As the slope narrows and lengthens (hence the "long-tail"), it begins containing things searched for at lower levels of volume.

Long-tail keywords are semi-related to a more important short-tail keyword. For example, one of Apple's main short-tail keywords is "smartphones." A long-tail they would build content around is "how mobile data uses GPS." This type of long-tail gives them space to feed their main keywords, while building up their blog and adding content to attract new customers.

This could be confusing because it branches out in so many different ways. The entire linking and keyword structure, including topic authority processes (as we discussed earlier), can be overwhelming. Fortunately, brands have found a way to control all of this using content clusters.

Content Clusters

When it comes to converting with content, the required foundation is based on content clusters. A content cluster visually maps out how a piece of content will be structured. Here are the specifics of how a cluster is created.

Think of a content cluster like the solar system. The sun is in the center—your target keyword (the main thing you are trying to build out). The outer planets revolving around the sun are keywords related to the main keyword, but with a slightly different angle. Using this structure, you can create content that aligns with the content cluster you have created. This helps the content-building process, increases site traffic, and improves domain authority.

Finally, note the content cluster helps develop subtopics and plot ones that are already planned. When you visually map out a cluster, ideas begin to formulate more clearly, and you can better serve the ultimate function, which is creating content that converts, which ultimately builds Brand Primacy.

In the same vein, brands take advantage of interactive content to further boost their primacy. As the name states, interactive content is something customers can interact with. This includes downloadable tools or content; however, it can be all types of things. For the sake of building Brand Primacy, we will focus on a very specific type of interactive content: the kind that offers users a chance to use or own a portion or part of a product/service. Let us use the popular Microsoft Office Suite as an example. Imagine if certain programs from the suite (like Microsoft Word, Excel, and PowerPoint) were free-to-use tools. By offering these tools individually for free, Microsoft lets users interact with the content of the main product one by one. This way, they can grab that specific traffic.

8

BLOWING THE CAP OFF INTENT

HOW EASY WOULD IT BE IF WE ALWAYS KNEW WHAT someone's intentions were? Conversely, think how difficult life would be if we never understood a person's intent. Unfortunately, we are generally in the dark when it comes to figuring out people's desires. Even when we think we know, we do not. For Google, this is true as well.

The system takes a stab in the dark using its databases of knowledge. Sometimes it is right, other times it is not (certainly we have all had searches that gave poor results). The good thing for brands is we do not necessarily need to understand the intent of a search. Rather, we need to understand the search intent when someone searches for specific keywords.

Here is an example that applies these concepts. Someone logs on to Google and searches for "digital data system." This is where things get interesting. What is their search intent? Are they looking to find brands that sell digital data systems? Do they want to know what a digital data system is? Do they want to know about different types of digital data software tools? Or, maybe they want to know what digital data is and the different types—multiple search intents. Brands are creating content around keywords to best fit the user's search intent.

Remember how I pointed out the importance of being the first brand that shows up in Google search results? I am going to dive deeper, giving you the ways to actually make it happen. Of course, it will not be easy. Chances are other brands are working just as hard.

However, it is 100 percent possible to outrank them and leave them wondering why they are no longer in first place. The answer lies in Brand Primacy, which is an unknown variable no amount of hard work can make up for. Your brand can achieve Brand Primacy, even if you think the competition is too fierce, or even if the brands are bigger and better.

My path to success in Brand Primacy in all my endeavors has always centered around coming up with concepts others were not willing to try. When some brands rest on their laurels, satisfied with their position, I take big chances instead. When some brands believe the "rules" of SEO are set in stone, I break them anyway. For me, I looked at SEO from an outsider's perspective, gauging it differently. This is where search intent comes into play, since it is such a big part of figuring out the SEO path of success.

Brands spent so much time catering to Google's algorithm they failed to focus on beating competitors and meeting what the algorithm demanded. I took things on from a different angle, pushing my teams to develop ways to answer the search intent call, and our content began smashing the competition and ranking first.

So how can you go about doing this? Let us examine the main factor in play here: search intent. It is the goal or objective of any search. The search intent is often a purchase, the answer to a question, or finding a specific site.

For example, if a user typed "cheapest mittens available", that search intent would be for a purchase. They can also type a question: "what year did the Yankees win the World Series?" Lastly, if they typed "Twitter" into the search, they are looking for the specific site. When it comes to Brand Primacy, our goal is to make our brand *the* recognized site as much as possible. For brands, this means many things. In the above example, if someone searched for "Twitter", it would be ideal for the Twitter website to be first in the rankings. That should be easy, since Google favors brands and feeds its users exactly what they want in searches. However, now it is time to branch out a little. How about searches for "tweets", "tweeting", "follow", or "retweet"—these are other things Twitter will want routed to their site. Going a step further, Twitter might also start showing up in searches for "language", "symbols", "connection", "digital communication", etc. Again though, this (ranking for these terms) should be easy to accomplish. We understand the most likely thing someone wants when they search for "tweeting" is Twitter content. The goal then is to find ways to make our content and domain branch out further and be the solution for a wider range of things. Using the above example again, the "cheapest mittens available" search, there are opportunities to be had in that type of search intent, even if you are not selling mittens. For one, you could know how to best answer the question, based on a combination of your authority (maybe your brand is heavy into clothing materials) and your content. For example, maybe one of the results users get fed is an article you wrote about the cheapest mittens available.

Now, here is where it gets interesting. Using a complex process, Google is designed to determine search intent based on different factors. In achieving Brand Primacy, we can use this to our advantage. Just as we learned brands have an edge over other results in Google's rankings, we should also recognize the power of search intent and how, if understood correctly, it can bring unlimited potential to brands. What does the user want? They want accurate search results. What are they searching for? Whatever it is, make sure your brand is the one who gives it to them.

Finally, take note that not even Google is perfect in this regard. Like many of you, I have had searches that do not deliver good results. It is frustrating, but it shows brands they can do better. They can improve to be part of the solution so no search ends with disappointment.

9

BRAND AWARENESS PLAYS A PART

WHENEVER WE AS CONSUMERS SEE A LOGO ON A PRODUCT, we have ideas about that product based on the characteristics of the brand behind the logo. For instance, we are more likely to trust the drink inside the plastic bottle if the logo is Gatorade instead of Frank's Sporty Drink—that is brand awareness.

Brand awareness is a measurement of how well people can recognize characteristics, qualities, and other aspects of a brand. The important thing to point out here is, if a brand has strong awareness, it is likely more popular than other brands.

Once Google determines search intent, they will feed specific brands to the top of the results based on the answer they provide. Only one of them will be first and that is where another layer of search intent comes into play: the influence of brand awareness on the searcher's intent. In this way, brand awareness has a direct impact on rankings. So, it stands to reason if you achieve brand awareness, you will position yourself to be served as the solution to search intent for a lot of different queries. This in turn, ultimately, builds Brand Primacy.

Here is an example to help illustrate where brand awareness comes into the equation of search intent. If I do a Google search for "marketing automation," the first brands we will likely see are Salesforce, Marketo, and (not surprisingly) HubSpot. Even though the main search intent is to find the definition of marketing automation, vendors (brands selling products) show up. And you do not see any listicles, review sites, or publishers—that is Google favoring brands.

Besides getting better at technical and content SEO, how can Salesforce, Marketo, and HubSpot distinguish themselves in this SERP? Well, brand association would help this. If marketers can connect the brand to the general search "marketing automation," then the general search is more likely to serve the brand because of the Google Knowledge Graph and user behavior. The user knows (perhaps subconsciously) that the brand is associated with the general search, so the user clicks on the brand. After this, Google feeds user behavior back into the algorithm and the next time, the brand most associated with marketing automation will come up at the top. That is the first layer of this process to keep in mind.

So, what types of things influence brand awareness? Fortunately, there is a bit to do if you are lagging in this area. To increase your brand awareness, you will need to take a very active approach. I will offer some basic strategies—the absolute fundamentals—followed by unique methods designed to help you create separation between yourself and other brands (or if you are behind them in the rankings, to close the gap).

Here are some effective options to improve it.

THE POWER OF PR

The first thing to consider is public relations (PR). Though this is a fundamental part of the process, there are brands who underutilize or misuse it. A PR campaign completes a specific task by informing the public of important, positive news about a brand. PR gives brands more attention, but it is more complex than that.

The complexity lies in determining how to angle PR to reach the right demographics, but this is just the start. A successful PR campaign, one that raises brand awareness, takes serious consideration and planning. Before doing anything, create a blueprint of the campaign.

Determine the Audience and How to Reach Them

Keep in mind your brand values and the way you want the campaign to portray the brand. Another thing to consider is the medium you wish to use for promotion. For example, a PR campaign that targets radio would make a lot of sense if most of your target demographic listens to the radio. Also, recognize that demographics change and so do trends. Evaluate the efficacy of your PR from time to time, or suffer the consequences of a PR campaign that does not reach its intended audience. Like the above example, if you are finding good PR success with radio, you might reach a point where you are not. Before checking if it is something on your end, realize it is more likely the fact radio is reaching fewer people, especially now that automobile driving is on the decline. This is just one example, but it is important. Finally, there is a balance that must be struck between brand and audience when it comes to PR. This balance is delicate and deals with the idea of self-promotion, usefulness, and creativity.

Be Useful to Customers Instead of Braggadocious

Any PR can be seen as self-promotion, as it toots your own horn. Make sure it brings usefulness to the table. For example, how does it help a potential customer to read about a brand winning a safety award? Instead of bragging about it, use the news to show why you will keep customers safe. A blanket statement of "We have won ten safety awards" is not likely to catch a customer's attention. However, making it personal or showing how you have been safe will. To turn customers' heads, keep brand bragging to a minimum.

Stay Creative Throughout

Creativity is a large part of PR. If a story is boring, audiences will dismiss it, even if it was relevant to their interests. Look for ways to keep things fresh and exciting. One option, which large brands use, is hiring a PR agency. The above tactics and strategies are a lot of work, so delegating the tasks to a PR firm is reasonable. They also give brands experienced specialists who understand what works within certain industries. If an agency is not an option, at the very least hire the right people who have shown the ability to keep public-facing situations positive.

THE ART OF THE GUEST BLOG

The mighty metal band Metallica is famous for their insane guitar riffs, mind-bending metal, and crowd-drawing concerts. But here is something lesser known about them:

they charge people to try out for their band. At one point it cost $1 million to try out for Metallica. Upon first glance, this seems backward. It is almost like a car dealership paying customers to own a new car. The reason Metallica does this and the power of the guest blog for brand awareness are the same: it is the value the guest gains. If Metallica's drummer quit today, they would *need* someone to fill his shoes; however, the band understands any new member gains huge advantages, the same way brands can gain brand awareness with a guest blog. So, on the one hand you are giving content for free to a company, and giving them plenty of benefits that come with having that content. But rather than monetary pay, you are being paid in awareness.

Guest blogging is an often overlooked, highly effective method, giving insight into your authority, voice, and general brand. It also has the added value of improving your backlink profile and overall domain and topic authority.

To maximize Brand Primacy, make sure each time you get the opportunity to guest blog, you treat it like it is the most important blog you have ever written. Writing content to build someone else's blog can be frustrating; however, think of it like a chance to show what you can offer to people who are not familiar with your blog or brand. Besides being free and a great promotional tool, guest blogging is also a way to spread your message to the right audience, increase social media potential, grow backlinks, and improve your writing.

We start the blog-building process the same way we began the PR process—by creating a blueprint for our approach. This requires thoughtful consideration of the strategies and processes needed for the blogs you will be writing. Next, you will want to narrow the focus of prospective blogs to contribute to—not every blog will be a good fit.

Be willing to accept guest blogging work you can find, but also give yourself room to say no if the situation warrants. One thing that helps is researching and analyzing current demographics. Ask yourself if they would be interested in hearing the topics you write about and determine whether they would read your brand's blog in the future. When coming up with a topic, make sure it is exciting, interesting, and fits nicely with the rest of the blog. When I guest blog, I like to reference and quote people of authority. I find bringing experts into a piece keeps readers interested, as they now believe you take on a large part of that authority yourself.

The final strategy is the simplest and most basic: create amazing content! After you receive permission to write a guest blog, locate the perfect audience, find a winning topic, and bring things home with a powerful piece of content.

Consider whether it has been done before, if you put your own spin on it, or if yours sounds like everyone else's. This is your chance to blow readers out of the water and lure them to your blog, building brand awareness.

Lastly, remember to branch out your efforts to reach more blogs, creating better chances to reach more people. Just like with PR, remember that since our audiences are changing, we need to evaluate where we are guest blogging and how we are managing those opportunities.

BOOSTING BRAND AWARENESS

Once you have begun building a basic level of brand awareness through PR and guest blogging, the next step is to expand upon this foundation with some dynamic awareness-boosting ideas. Attack this step from all angles to ensure Google views your brand as superior, allowing you to reach your ultimate goal of Brand Primacy.

To begin, let us take a look at YouTube, which is owned by Google. Before going any further, note that Google favors YouTube videos in search queries. It, therefore, makes a lot of sense to create and build a branded YouTube channel, to both further our brand awareness and compound a lot of the SEO efforts that have gone into helping us rank in search. A well-constructed channel should act as an extension of a brand, building authority, informing target markets of products and services, and promoting brand awareness.

Similar to our PR and guest blogging efforts, the content of these videos needs to be interesting and high quality, otherwise it will not raise awareness. Hire the right people to make this happen.

Next, make sure you have things like newsletters to keep your brand circulating in people's minds from time to time.

Finally, remember creative, on-topic content is favored by Google the same way they favor authentic brands over hoaxy sites. To win Google's favor, we need to create powerful, original content.

This extends further than PR and guest blogging efforts. Brands often fail to adhere to this rule, instead falling victim to the idea that more is better. Though it is important to have a wide-ranging group of content, it is better to rein it in a little to focus on making sure it is strong. Audiences will take notice, and Google will as well.

When it comes to writing valuable content, note the layout, structure, messaging, voice, and anything else you value. Some of the most successful brands with elite Brand Primacy do not put out content every day, instead focusing on making what they do release...amazing.

The above strategies are designed to help you build brand awareness. In turn, building brand awareness helps you win the all-important battle for Google's search intent, which ultimately boosts your Brand Primacy.

Because you are a brand, you are already at a huge advantage. If your brand name is Salesforce, Marketo, or HubSpot, chances are you will rank higher than other websites for marketing automation, simply because the search intent algorithm rewards brands associated with the general search, ranking them higher. Now, in your industry, it is up to you to beat out other brands associated with general search terms. And we have shown how to do this, with the careful construction of brand awareness.

So, how does it all translate into ranking? Where does the algorithm gather the idea that, since your brand awareness is better, you deserve to rank higher? It all boils down to how users interact with the results. Let us circle back to our marketing automation example.

If HubSpot improved its brand awareness, it would signal to Google that it deserves to move up. Users would have to access it more. When searching for marketing automation, they would select it before anything else, and not close it immediately. Similarly, people who click into the top-ranking marketing automation website might click out right away when they realize (even subconsciously) it is not what they were looking for.

Knowing this, how should they go about accomplishing it? They know in order to win the search intent war, they need users to click their content more in search and keep it open. What are some ways we can go about making this happen? First, let us figure out how to make users click our brand instead of others.

THE KEYS TO BRAND RECOGNITION

If brand recognition holds so much sway over the outcome of Google search rankings, we should be bending over backward to improve it. Brand recognition is how well someone can identify a brand without seeing or hearing its name. Similar to awareness, brand recognition can help you win user clicks, since it ensures people will have your brand on their minds.

This is the result of them knowing a brand's color schemes or logo. To improve your recognition, work on staying consistent, creating memorable visual elements, and making unique audio logos or jingles.

This indirectly increases standing in the search engines, since better recognition boosts the chance to serve people who need your products or services. For example, if 1,000 people needed to buy hammers, and 850 of them easily recognized your brand when they searched for "hammers", they would select your brand over others. This increases the chances of your brand ranking first overall.

Building better brand recognition is a comprehensive effort that does not happen overnight. Focus on one thing and improve it, then move to the next. For example, consider your logo. Is it the right brand color? Does it truly represent your core values? Is it unique? In what ways does it speak to the customer? You would be surprised at how much detail goes into a brand logo. Even the font needs to be considered for the logo to fit with the rest of the design. Schedule some recurring checks to ensure the logo is not the problem. Like we have mentioned plenty now: things change.

Trends are trendy. Your logo should not need constant updates, nor should your other visual elements, but take note every so often. Now, take the next step and do the same with things like audio and other visual elements. And remember, the overarching key when working on these elements is consistency. It is okay to change them, but they need to be consistent across all channels. And remember, your logo shows up often in the SERPs.

Finally, the second part of the search intent equation is keeping users on your page once they click on it. Many different factors come into play here, one of which is we must immediately show the user our brand is the right one.

Whatever problem they have, we need to quickly offer a perfect solution. Think of your content like a timeshare pitch—people either forgo it altogether or hold their breath until it is over. Make sure your "pitch" does not remind users of the timeshare event, where a carrot is dangled in front of them.

Just get to the good stuff right away and elaborate. No one wants to be toyed with. This does not mean we ever expect to retain users on our page if they were not looking for our product or service. For example, with the marketing automation search, someone looking for a marketing automation solution will not stay on a webpage for an immediate software pitch, no matter how good the pitch might be. We need to give them the info they are looking for up front, then pitch later.

And that means we need to retain users who are looking for what we offer. If the visitor does not feel we are the right fit, they will bounce off the page and Google will adjust accordingly. Another thing to consider is the appearance and performance of our page. If it is slow, the user will exit, no matter how good our product or service.

If the page looks outdated or cluttered, they will leave. This needs to be measured and analyzed from a mobile perspective as well. A functional website is not functional if it only works well for a desktop. Lastly, and most importantly, if it is not brand-consistent, they will leave.

Imagine searching for "soda" and clicking on the Coca-Cola result, going to their home page, and seeing a bunch of blue and purple. Because of Coca-Cola's very popular red logo and themes, you would think you clicked the wrong brand. When you consider and piece together all of this, you will increase the chance for the search intent to ultimately favor you.

Circling back to my success in fighting for Brand Primacy, I always come to the same conclusion about how I did it: I took the angle others were not taking. This meant maximizing both the technical and content side of the SEO equation. This will not always work, but when it came to search intent, it did—because other brands were faltering. Hopefully this serves as a lesson for you in the ever-changing world of SEO: if you notice weaknesses in your competitor's approaches, do not try to beat them by making the same mistakes.

When everything comes together—brand awareness, SEO, etc.—you have a good chance at satisfying the search intent in Google, which is something a lot of brands are concerned with and fighting to do these days. Fortunately, you have an advantage over many brands, because not all are aware of the importance of Brand Primacy, nor do they know how to fight for it.

In the next chapter, we will further your brand building with strategies to increase overall consistency.

10

DOMAIN AUTHORITY

HOW EXPERTISE DRIVES TRAFFIC

IT IS A CONCEPT AS OLD AS TIME: THE RICH GET RICHER. We see this in action when a millionaire leverages his or her wealth into becoming a billionaire. The same thing applies to domain authority, as larger, well-established brands leverage their rankings "wealth" into greater wealth. Keep this idea in mind going forward, because the basic principle behind it necessitates consistent observance for success.

The most successful brands are winning in Brand Primacy by building domain authority. There are many different nuances to this, but the core ideas are easy to understand.

WHAT IS DOMAIN AUTHORITY?

Domain authority is a term coined by Moz, which refers to how well a website relates to a subject area or industry, and how this relation impacts its search engine rankings.

Though it is relatively difficult to predict how Google measures a domain, there are a few tried and true factors that have legitimate effects on the process. In our discussion of rankings and primacy, we have already roughly touched on a few.

Branded Search Traffic

One factor Google considers is the amount of searches a brand receives. This means if a user types "popcorn" into the search, is looking for a brand called *Popcorn,* and clicks on their site, that counts toward that brand's domain authority.

A Brand's Social Influence

As a brand's content becomes more prevalent on different social media platforms, Google takes notice. Unfortunately for smaller, newer brands, length of existence plays a role, and rightfully so.

For example, imagine if Google's algorithm agreed a six-month-old brand should be the authority on computer technology and hardware over a brand like Intel. Users searching for information on computing would much rather be served by the Intel blog.

Since this is the case, the overall length of time a brand has been around will play a role. Brands who have been there longer than yours will get preference. Does that mean you cannot catch up? Of course not. But it will take time. Consider the other factors—such as link building, increasing rankings, etc.—and focus on them as well.

Links

The biggest factor when determining domain authority is links. We already discussed links, pointing out the problems with companies who tried to game Google using back-link-buying strategies.

This applies here too, as the algorithm favors brands that link to quality sites and vice versa. The types of links matter as well (quality links are great, but if you are only getting links from one source, the quality becomes irrelevant). Similarly, the quantity of links matters, but not nearly as much as the quality.

All of the above information runs into another age-old question: which came first, the chicken or the egg? We do not know the answer, but we do know how brands build domain authority.

HOW ARE BRANDS BUILDING AUTHORITY?

The primary way brands build domain authority is by answering questions from searches on Google around what their product does. For instance, HubSpot does marketing automation—they solve the search intent for marketing topics.

If a user asks Google, "What is email management?" Google might send them to a HubSpot article that answers this question in great detail. The different topics HubSpot solves the search intent for increase HubSpot's standing in domain authority. HubSpot knows people are searching for things like "What is email management?" because they do analytics-based research on search traffic. What HubSpot and other brands are doing is building content suited for Google. They cover a wide range of topic areas related to or loosely related to what the brand does. Brands like HubSpot have begun building content for Google at scale. This means they are expanding the amount of content they create and attempting to corner each keyword ranking slot. However, they do fall victim to the idea of quality over quantity.

HubSpot and other brands are doing this by building topic clusters around key knowledge areas. Let us consider a cluster HubSpot uses to build domain authority around marketing automation: email management. HubSpot built multiple email management topic areas targeting searches like "email management tips," "email list management," "email marketing guide," and many more.

HubSpot has tens of thousands of blog articles relating to everything they do. Each article builds domain authority for them because of the search rankings they provide. That is what made them one of the top domains in the world. They achieved Brand Primacy in one of the toughest areas of general search. They are the top-ranking brand for keywords such as "marketing automation", "marketing automation software", and every other important general search term related to their product. And HubSpot is more likely to rank for these over non-vendor websites thanks to Brand Primacy.

As I mentioned above, the quality and quantity of links a brand has in their content is important. Another valuable part of this is backlinks, which result when an article links to a brand and its content. This is not something brands control, but they encourage it by creating strong content.

Using the above example of HubSpot, let us say a large, well-trusted brand was writing an article for a new product or service they created. They needed an expert to link out to concerning email management, since that could affect the new product. They google "email management", see HubSpot's article as first in the ranking, read it, and link to it since their readers could benefit. This is an example of a good backlink and the process of building brand authority effectively in action.

Increasing domain authority boils down to two things: giving Google users a good experience and solving for their search intent. This relationship is harmonious, and these two things build off one another to increase a brand's domain authority. A brand needs to position its content around solving all types of search intent related to its main expertise. Then, they have to make sure each piece of content provides a great user experience so the user does not immediately leave the page.

The above concepts build off one another, and they require serious attention. Therefore, meticulously compare your current strategy to see if it matches these ideas. If it does not, improve upon it, because there are benefits that come along with building domain authority, particularly what it can mean for brands.

WHAT DOES THIS MEAN FOR BRANDS?

Building domain authority is how many brands achieve Brand Primacy. When they provide a good experience for Google around their topic area, Google deems their domain an authority in that realm. Their top- and bottom-of-the-funnel general search rankings go up.

Think of this concept like learning algebra. To learn it, you need to understand many different steps and principles. You do not learn it by looking up the definition of the word "algebra". To be an expert or an authority in the field of algebra, you would have to be skilled in all the different nuances and functions of the mathematical language.

Now apply this to brands trying to achieve Brand Primacy. Let us say a brand wants to be an authority on wood, which they sell on their website. Would they accomplish this by writing one article about wood? Probably not. Similar to our algebra example, this is the equivalent of learning the definition. Instead, they would need a comprehensive group of content that focuses on wood, different kinds of wood, where it comes from, different strategies about wood carving, wood storage, etc.

The more they can branch out (no pun intended), the better equipped they will be to be an authority in the eyes of Google. However, a brand cannot become an authority simply by creating a blog and writing articles about many minor topics. Instead, they need to write engaging, thoughtful content on these minor topics (as well as provide a legitimate service with quality wood, customer service, etc.). Remember, Google wants content that provides the user with a great experience in addition to answering their search intent.

The above example should be exciting for brands. Essentially, Google is telling brands they will rate them as experts and place their content high in the rankings, above actual experts, simply because they have built domain authority.

For example, imagine an expert woodworker who knows about wood in great detail. She creates a blog about wood, but her articles rank lower on Google, below a brand that sells wood, despite this brand using copywriters who do not know nearly as much about wood to write their articles.

Not only has Google effectively boosted the brand's business big time over the independent woodworker, but Google has also made the brand the expert, indirectly, by suggesting its content is to be trusted over everyone else's. It truly is an exciting time to be a brand. Brands can win the general search traffic game in both the top of the funnel and bottom of the funnel simply by building domain authority.

REAPING WHAT YOU SOW, SO TO SPEAK

Going back to our HubSpot example, by competing on Google, and playing their game, they dominated SERPs, gained relevant traffic, and made more sales than their competitors.

HubSpot's annual recurring revenue is about $1 billion while their top competitor, Marketo (before being sold to Adobe), was $400 million. This provides a concrete example to point to, which is tough to undercut or poke holes in. This is a direct result of adhering to the principles of Brand Primacy.

Brands can also remarket to the audience, feeding specific customers content based on past behaviors. And who better to take care of this than Google? Google Ads is the second-largest display advertising platform globally, and remarketing audiences are important to any Google Ads account. By bringing in more relevant traffic to a domain, it increases the remarketing audience.

For instance, by getting users to click on a HubSpot article from Google, they give them a cookie and remarket to them. These remarketing audiences are further segmented to make them more accurate in Google Ads. This is cheaper than sending out display ads using an audience builder. I found this out firsthand, as I used to run display and video ads on Google, LinkedIn, and YouTube. I found by implementing these accuracy efforts, it cost one-third less to get the same number of leads/sales.

Brands also get another big benefit from building domain authority: brand recognition from a relevant audience. Searchers finding email management articles on HubSpot see that the article came from HubSpot. The logo even appears in the SERPs for many searches.

Audiences who read this content, especially if they find it helpful, will likely see HubSpot in a positive light. Many also share the content with the social buttons that appear on every HubSpot article (consider putting these features in your own content). Therefore, building domain authority in this way goes beyond brand recognition to brand engagement.

Brands get a lot from playing Google's game. Providing great content for their search audience gives them new business and high-quality brand engagement.

11

A DEEP DIVE INTO BACKLINKS

BY FAVORING BRANDS TO HIT THE TOP OF THE SERPs, Google guarantees their own long-term survival, as the top domains base themselves on Google's own algorithm. It becomes a circular and mutual effect. So long as brands adhere to ranking practices, Google remains in fashion.

And top results are more likely to get more backlinks. This occurs because so many websites find it useful to link to a certain site within their content. The more top results a domain has for general terms, the more likely it will have a ton of domain authority.

Google accepts that brands will have a fundamental advantage and permanently change the authority landscape, while also changing Google itself. Furthermore, when these high-ranking brands gather more backlinks, they continue to stay at the top.

The preferential attachment model underpins this. For those unfamiliar with the preferential attachment process, it is the idea that the rich get richer. Why do the top domains get backlinks? Because they are the top domains. It is a paradoxical loop that has found a way to affect SEO and requires observance for brands to succeed, no matter which part of the model they may find themselves in.

When I was doing content management for software companies, I would get alerts on big domains that backlinked to my articles. Oddly enough, I would get backlinks from *The New York Times, The Washington Post,* and the *Guardian.* Surprised, I would Google the anchor they used to link to my article and sure enough, my articles ranked first for those search terms. The editor at those publications had likely googled the term and linked the top result, which, to them, seemed like the most authoritative (likely because it ranked first in Google). Many backlinks from authoritative publications simply go to the top ranking for the anchored text.

This becomes self-perpetuating from a societal standpoint as well. Reinforcement of the brand as an authority through Brand Primacy further legitimizes those brands.

This improves clickthrough rate for search terms and the cycle continues.

Initially, links were a way to connect semi-related and related pages on the web together. Google discovered there was a more efficient way, and their search utilized linking differently. They realized the user experience was better with less random links. Also, the more legitimate links connected to a domain from other publications, the easier it was for Google to push them toward the users.

For brands, this remains a large part of what drives Brand Primacy. Google's algorithm honors the idea that a good link from a trusted brand deserves notice, which results in strengthened rankings. When building and bettering a domain's SEO, different things can be done to optimize. This is important, but it is not the only consideration in terms of links.

THE SNOWBALL EFFECT OF BACKLINKS

The phrase "the rich keep getting richer" has a lot of truth to it. A wealthy person has access to investment vehicles most do not. Websites (domains) are no different. Larger domains are able to rank for more terms. When they rank for these, other domains are more likely to link to them. As a consequence, large domains continue to get bigger due to their comparative advantage.

For example, if a domain ranks for the term "marketing automation," other domains related to this term will link visitors to the most authoritative website. How do editors determine which resource is the most authoritative? The same way everyone else does: google it and view the top result as the most authoritative. In most cases, the editor will link their audience there. The domain that ranks first will be reinforced with more backlinks, making it more authoritative in Google and more likely to rank first. It is then easier for the domain that ranks first for "marketing automation" to rank for long-tail keywords or related terms.

It is no surprise that Brand Primacy has a snowball effect. Even a slight advantage allows brands to build a ton of momentum. All brands need to do is begin building it to gain an incredible competitive advantage in Google.

There are also branching-out possibilities related to Brand Primacy. Using long-tail to gain an advantage with higher-value short-tail terms is a good strategy given that related backlinks come through the long-tail and leverage the short-tail. This shows how important it is for larger domains to attack the long-tail to keep other domains at bay.

Backlinks gained from authoritative brands are even more valuable. Brands should prioritize getting backlinks from other brands. There are a few good ways to do this. One is by mentioning a service a brand provides and communicating the article to the brand. There are other backlink procurement programs that are often effective. Outreach is important. Having original research that brands want to link to is the most effective in my experience. For instance, you can do research with the audience of brands that provide "marketing automation" software and get trends they are focusing on that year. This can then be linked to by marketing automation service providers to show their audience what their peers are currently focusing on.

12

VIDEO, MEET SEARCH

LET US NOW EXAMINE ONE OF THE FASTEST-GROWING, lesser-known ways to build domain authority: videos, specifically YouTube videos.

Not enough brands are aware of the impact a YouTube channel can have on their business. Its importance cannot be overstated. Why is it so valuable? Partly because it can further Brand Primacy if done in conjunction with a solid blog content strategy.

I do not expect brands will be unopposed on the platform—competitors will have accounts as well, and they will fight for rankings and customers—but not enough competitors are on YouTube. The reality is brands should be battling each one of their competitors for rankings and finding new customers on YouTube, but it is rarely happening. This is like discovering a gold mine. Do not miss out on this brief period in time, before everyone catches on. Also, do not overestimate your presence on the platform if you are already established—stagnation is possible.

In fact, a past company I worked for had great rankings for our industry, and I led the charge pivoting to target YouTube. This helped us gain YouTube search traffic for our topics. And, once we had views and subscribers, we linked the platform to our website and got leads. In the topic area we built, tens of thousands of views came in the first six months, which helped us get more sales.

Now let us dive into how brands use YouTube to build authority. Remember, to gain traction, it is important to rank on Google search for different important keywords. What if YouTube could help in this area? When done right, it can.

You can create videos based on topics of new articles, and link them (the video and article). This creates a greater chance to gain traffic on that specific article, which will increase its Google ranking, which then boosts domain authority.

Another way a YouTube account boosts domain authority is through traffic from links on the profile. When a user sees a video, they may click the profile and head to the brand's website. Keep in mind the power the presence of a YouTube channel can have for a brand. It would be strange if a company like Apple did not have a YouTube account. It seems like a given, because why would such a popular company not scoop up that extra traffic and reach out to new markets? When you consider the obvious benefits video traffic brings, it is clear why brands are utilizing it.

BUILDING YOUR OWN YOUTUBE PROFILE

Now that you know why a YouTube account is important and how it can build your domain authority, let us make sure you do everything correctly. Even if you are a brand that already has a business YouTube profile, this section will be beneficial. Are you getting everything you should out of your account? Is it bringing the customers and traffic you hoped for? If not, let us make a few adjustments.

We will begin with the actual account or profile. There are two different options here, because you are either a brand that already has a YouTube account or a brand that does not.

To feed two birds with one scone, I will list the important factors required to build a strong YouTube profile:

1. **Brand consistency.** First, focus on brand element consistency. If your brand website is filled with green colors and sharp layouts, a

YouTube profile with blue colors and curved layout images makes little sense. Keep things consistent so the transition from clicking the YouTube link to the website is seamless. On that note, also make sure there is a link to your website and other social media sites. YouTube is a great way to get your brand out there and inform customers of new products and services, but it is not great for communication between the customer and the brand. These links provide a way to get in touch.

2. **Featured channels.** Next, be sure to use the "featured channels" section to promote your sub-channels (if you have them) or similar helpful channels. Featured channels define your brand's place in the market by offering other videos related to your goals.

3. **The "about" section.** The final thing we need to touch on is the "about" section, which gives us a chance to detail our brand for new customers. When users finish watching our videos, they will want to know more about the brand who filmed it. This will lead them to the "about" section, where they will want to know what the brand does. By giving them a clear description with on-point

messaging, you will inform them and lead them to check you out further. Make sure your "about" page delivers.

Lastly, remember Google owns YouTube. Google purchased YouTube and will favor a YouTube video when offering videos on a Google search. As I have written throughout this book: Google is not fair. This is being proven repeatedly by all sorts of publications, who find Google is promoting YouTube videos in results even when they are not the "best" option. Do not expect them to be neutral or unbiased, because they are not, so take advantage.

THE BENEFITS OF HAVING A BUSINESS YOUTUBE CHANNEL

Just like writing articles to rank, your videos should follow similar guidelines. User experience is important. As more people watch and interact (commenting, sharing, etc.) with your videos, rankings will increase, and your videos will be featured higher on the results.

To perfect this, consider the topics and the best ways to professionally discuss them in an informative manner. Is what you are delivering giving the user something new and teaching them the basics of the keyword? It is easy to check on the other videos about a topic to see what your competition left out. Find ways to differentiate so the user does not click off your video within thirty seconds, or worse, does not open it at all. Another thing to consider is length. If you are uploading a webinar or interview, the time length is irrelevant, and will reach thirty minutes to one hour quite easily. However, your other videos need to be adapted to how much the user is willing to sit through.

Think of your own time online—how much of a video do you watch? Are there certain lengths you avoid? A good sweet spot is three to five minutes, depending on what you are promoting or trying to explain. It is important to let the viewers know they will be getting something new, interesting, and important immediately in the video so they do not exit, which lowers the ranking.

Also consider the fact that YouTube offers a new and exciting way to connect with target audiences. Making a connection by reading an article is unlikely, no matter how good the article is. However, the connection is much more likely when you put a face in front of the camera. Customers can see a brand representative in human form, which lets them think differently about your brand and its ideals.

Finally, think about the ways to create your videos. What types of things work best for certain topics? If an illustration or cartoon works, go for that. Resources may limit you, but that does not mean you cannot find ways to put out content that fits customer needs.

If you have built an article that explains something very well, but the readers tend to lose focus, a video on the article might keep their attention longer. This is not an attempt for the video to be pulled onto Google; it is a way to improve the clarity of your article. As such, the video has no reason to be on the YouTube platform if you do not want it to be.

Though other video platforms are less favored by Google, the point is you are improving the ranking indirectly, through content building, which increases the overall success of the article. Think of ways to improve and supplement your content on different pieces, such as articles and blog posts, with a creative video. This will lead to stronger domain authority.

13

UNDERSTANDING, THEN OUTRANKING THE COMPETITION

NOW IT IS TIME TO CONSIDER HOW TO PASS BRANDS IN THE rankings, especially when they are bigger and more established than you.

A common occurrence in movies is when a person, company, etc., is up against all odds. The sentiment "they are too big to compete with" is met with someone willing to try. When I reference "brand superiors" throughout this book, I mean brands with bigger domains and better Google rankings.

The good thing about Brand Primacy is Google rankings do not reflect which brand is biggest (both in terms of domain and popularity). Instead, there are other factors, part of a comprehensive system of elements, that all lead to search rankings. Our goal is to knock them down a peg and overtake them in all the important keywords.

The reality is our brand cannot always be top dog (biggest domain, largest financial backing, etc.). Sometimes, we are at a disadvantage to bigger and more resourceful brands. When the difference between us and brand superiors is overwhelming, special tactics are required to achieve Brand Primacy.

If you remember my story from the Introduction, you will know I came from a place of underdog as well—an English major and writer in a world of business grads, working at a company with a smaller domain than many of the "big guys." Throughout my quest to rank on Google for numerous important keywords, I had to seek out bigger and more financially substantial brands with more expansive domains as targets to attack. I used the tactics below to chip away at them.

UNDERSTANDING YOUR COMPETITION

First things first, you cannot get anywhere without a true understanding of your competing brands, especially the ones outranking you on Google.

It is not enough to compile a list of brand names beating you. Instead, there needs to be in-depth details that guide you to decisions in these processes. Here are some things to consider:

- First, what has your brand superior done to get where they are? What were their strategies? You might not be able to pinpoint this exactly, but with a little research, you can come awfully close.

- What kind of content do they write? How do they behave on different social media platforms?

- Recognize what type of advantages this superior brand has over yours. If you opened a burger restaurant, you would be able to point out how McDonald's is different.

- Similarly, how does your brand superior differ? Are they a massive company? Is their domain authority massive?

These types of details help us formulate a plan. We want to land a knockout blow, but they are the favorites, so we cannot enter the ring throwing haymakers. We need to look for a tiny weakness—particularly in their attempts at maintaining Brand Primacy—and slowly pick away, until it rips wide open. The following tips will put you in the position to do so.

TARGETING COMPETITORS SPECIFICALLY

This section is of the utmost importance because it sets you up for long-term success using strategies no one else understands or implements.

Most brands only consider themselves when attempting to rank on Google. They think in terms of "How can we do this well?" This is acceptable, but it will only deliver mediocre results. The other half of this battle is attacking our opponents directly.

Brands should also consider competitors. This is not limited to checking out how top-ranking brands are doing it and falling in line, either. Instead, it is finding those at the top and going directly at them, declaring war on their success and spot in the rankings.

If you rank behind several different brand superiors, it will help if you choose the one directly in front of you and attempt to overtake them in the Google rankings.

Think of it like running a race: if you are behind many people, try to move ahead of one first. Then the next, and so on until you are in first place. This is a lengthy process, but you are in the driver's seat thanks to the favor brands are given in Google.

Here is an exercise that will begin to build your overall potential and solidify your brand. Find a brand superior that is similar to yours—similar domain authority, size, etc. Preferably, pick one who barely outranks you on important search terms (use either an SEO tool to check this, or simply search for the keyword in an incognito browser window on Google).

If you are fifth in the rankings, they should be fourth. Now, start picking them apart piece by piece. Undoubtedly, they have mistakes in many areas. Locate these mistakes by reviewing their content and the technical aspects of it. Learn from these mistakes. Research everything about them. Find ways to outdo them and go for it. For example, if a competitor has written an article that only briefly answers the search intent, write a competing article that answers it better. Let us say they have written an article on data storage. The information is comprehensive, but pretty dry, uneventful, and unappealing. You write an even more comprehensive article about data storage with a unique voice, more examples, new sections, and an angle toward the current year, or a topical situation the reader will relate to. If nothing else, you will know you have put out an article more people will enjoy reading, even if ranking for data storage is not your top priority. You will be surprised how much this will help, and even more surprised at the fact not many competitors will fight back (because they are not yet aware of the importance of Brand Primacy). Because of the intricacies of SEO, so many brands are behind in these areas, and once you pass them, they never come back.

HELPFUL TACTICS

If you could overtake brand superiors instantly, that would be the best solution, but it is impossible. Instead, aim to do the little things better than your opponents, one at a time. Once they react, you will have already taken the legs out from under them and achieved Brand Primacy.

Everyone struggles to get this part right: you will not beat them at their own game. Remember, you are the underdog. You are playing with half a deck of cards and they are the house. If you try to be them, you will lose to them. It is that simple. Instead, you need to differentiate by digging deeper into the smaller details they overlook. For example, go after some keyword rankings they did not evaluate or overlooked. This is going to take hours of research and creativity. In what ways can you offer audiences something different than your brand superiors?

It used to be common to avoid keywords deemed "hard" to rank for in popular SEO tools. If it is too difficult to rank for, why bother? This was the mindset, and still is the mindset, of your industry competitors. Instead of rolling up their sleeves and attacking the problem, they back away from it and leave it to everyone else to fight over. There is a time when you will not want to enter the fray of a tough keyword, but if it is one you need, go for it. The one thing you will have over the competition is the fact that you know they are avoiding it. They are not even in the game you will be playing. This is a huge advantage and a strategy to carry with you at all times.

Blog/Article Tips

Let us say an imaginary brand, Brand A, has a massive domain authority, tons of backlinks, etc. They create a blog section for "customer experience" and write fifty different blog posts for it. A Google search for "customer experience" offers Brand A's "Guide to Customer Experience" blog post as the featured snippet (which makes it the top result).

More importantly, the ranking second, third, and fourth brands have all copied Brand A, creating nearly identical articles—they simply changed the logos, some of the writing, and layouts. This is always going to get outranked, since they are creating a lesser version of the original. If all the brands create a "Guide to Customer Experience" blog post, the biggest domain wins. You need to attack the mundane with a piece that turns heads.

Start with the title; you could introduce a new idea or anything else that makes it stand out without being too salesy. For example, how about "5 Customer Experience Trends in 2022"? And do not think a simple title change will get the job done. The content itself needs to be extremely engaging, easy to read, and unique. I will not get too much into detail concerning that, but here are some quick things to consider:

Break up the text. Do not overthink this, as there is little rhyme or reason behind it. Most people looking for an article are skimming over the content anyway, even if they have discovered exactly what they were looking for in their search. When they open your article, do not meet them with a giant brick of text. They will not want to read it. A few sentences will draw them in much better.

Include pictures/bulleted lists. Images are great because they make the article more accessible, offer a fresh dynamic, and give readers something to look at when scrolling through the piece. Bulleted lists are great because they bring structure to the article, especially for readers skipping large portions of it.

Make your intros stand out. Just as huge text chunks drive readers away, a weak intro will as well. Think of it like this: your meta title entices them to click the article in the first place. The intro then convinces them to read the rest of the article. If it is boring or a bit off-topic, they are hitting the "back" button and clicking another article, which is a devastating result for your brand in terms of the Google algorithm.

Make sure your subheadings are intriguing. As I have pointed out, the average internet user does not read an entire article. Chances are good most people will see your title, intro, and a few H2s (subheadings). You must make your header title powerful, interesting, and challenging to the reader. It has to promise them something they have never heard of before. And of course, make sure you meet the title of your subheading with the content. Do not leave your reader hanging with some frustrating clickbait.

Another reason to craft good H2s is they are often taken by Google and placed on the SERP as the main part of a featured snippet.

USING KEYWORD DISRUPTION EFFECTIVELY

Now that you have some basics on differentiating content, let us discuss another way to overcome the advantage brand superiors have: keyword disruption. Keyword disruption is a focused attack on a single keyword. It is the equivalent of attacking a small undefended fortress instead of rushing for the king.

Through your research, you will find brand superiors have some keywords they rank well for on Google. In fact, many of their articles will internally link to the main piece, giving it more strength.

This tactic is like a guerilla warfare attack on brand superior keywords. You do not want to go head-on with the main army at first. Instead, find and go after a weak point.

They cannot possibly focus their efforts on every single keyword, and it is not in their best interest to anyway. But this gives you a chance to make a move. Find a way to outrank them for something they do not structure their content around. The more you do this, the weaker their overall grip on Brand Primacy becomes.

Before they know it, you will have sprouted up on their radar, but the wheels will already be in motion. You will no longer be a brand that does not even scratch the surface; you will be a direct competitor. From here, it is anyone's ball game. Why not yours?

FINDING THE RIGHT KEYWORDS TO FOCUS ON

The next tactic to consider is the type of keywords to attack. Like going after smaller brands, you should go after smaller keywords. Why is this so important? For reasons we discussed earlier in the chapter, you can make a huge dent on brand superiors without facing them head-on.

This method gives you a chance to indirectly fight them, by going after things they have not yet discovered or do not care for. This way, you build an entire group of keywords to rank for without ever combatting the big guys.

So, how do you go about this? First, it is going to take some research. Look for keywords your competition is not ranking for (or better yet, does not write content for). This is best done in an SEO tool like Ahrefs or Moz, but Google is a good enough resource. Next, find keywords that would not be hard to rank for. Side note: if the keywords your brand needs to rank for are considered "very hard" to rank for, you still need to attempt it. High competition is part of the process.

Remember, you are the underdog and need to find things you can manage. So, what kinds of things fall into this category? To find out, create a Google search for the keywords you have in mind. The ones that are dominated by things such as forum responses or publishers are ripe for the picking. These keywords are easy to rank for because there is not a lot of good content behind them and because Google favors brands. The Google algorithm was unable to find something well written by a brand concerning them, so they have resorted to a forum post or publisher to make do. A well-written piece will beat them, and you can do this repeatedly while building an army of keywords, growing your domain, and giving you a chance to go after bigger keywords.

Before we get overexcited about these unique possibilities, let us make sure we have the right tools to navigate the state of SEO today. I am sure you have been given conflicting SEO advice in the past, so I want to give you clarity in these areas, particularly in how they relate to Brand Primacy.

14

TO HEED OR NOT
COMMON SEO ADVICE

Any new entrant into the world of SEO faces a mountain of technical information on topics like XML sitemaps, pagination rules, robots.txt files, rel=canonicals, and much more. This is true of publications, forums, influencer channels, YouTube videos, and conferences.

The first SEO conference I attended discussed whether XML sitemaps are cascading (in case anyone is wondering, they are). All of these technical SEO issues are very important, and they are the focus of the industry. The problem for most brands is they should at most be a minor focus. Instead, the main concern should be taking advantage of Brand Primacy by, for example, building domain authority with content.

There is a good reason why technical SEO is the main focus of SEO publications, conferences, and discourse. Most of the SEOs who advance to prominent positions in-house or in agencies deal with highly specialized issues. This might not apply to you, as you are looking to advance a brand in the Google rankings.

For instance, someone in-house at an e-commerce site might have hundreds of thousands of pages. How Google understands the structure of that site is vital for potential customers to find the right information.

If your site sells a type of T-shirt with three different colors and five sizes, you cannot have Google see all these pages equally—you must pick one and send users to it. Doing this tens of thousands of times with a revolving inventory is highly complex and necessitates a level of SEO expertise far beyond what is needed to achieve Brand Primacy in most industries.

One issue with putting technical SEO at the forefront of a Brand Primacy initiative is brands already have a built-in advantage on Google. On the other hand, publishers, site aggregators, or system rating websites have little room for error. For them, technical SEO needs to be perfect. Not only are they competing with brands who have a built-in advantage over them, but they have other domain competitors who are good at SEO. This means they have to hire an in-house SEO team and use technical agencies. In my work with an SEO publisher, we had eight full-time technical

SEO colleagues who only focused on optimizing for a team of twenty-five editors. Essentially, technical SEO is more important for the underdogs (those not benefiting from Brand Primacy).

Technical SEO is important but building domain authority with content first is a better approach. If you focus on technical SEO fixes first, hire an agency, and learn about the subject, years later you will be in the same place because you do not have content. This is because the technical side of SEO is only one piece, and you cannot improve without the rest of the puzzle. If, instead, you build the content first and do the technical fixes later, you could see an immediate boost from your domain-building activities. Also, the landscape of a domain changes drastically after implementing new content and campaigns. As a result, a lot of technical fixes need to be redone, doubling the workload.

By focusing on a content-first strategy, learning SEO is easier. The technical SEO issues are easily conceptualized when you have the baseline knowledge to solve for search intent from a content perspective. This is the "crawl before you can walk" version of the SEO world.

It is not that creating strong SEO content is any easier than solving technical SEO issues, but in terms of the types of prerequisites required to do one or the other, creating content is further removed from SEO, and thus easier to handle first. They build off each other, and it is important to note you will get a stronger grasp of both by successfully managing and learning about one, because of how they eventually intertwine.

One last thing to point out here—there is a vast wealth of knowledge and information about SEO available today, but it is often flawed, misrepresented, or outdated. Even some of the most trusted SEO experts give information that does not hold up to scrutiny or have published guides that are no longer valid (older guides are not necessarily useless, but consider the ever-changing landscapes of Google and imagine how hard it is to lock down an understanding of the moving parts). So, since there is misleading or unhelpful information about SEO out there, make sure you are aware of the most common errors.

THE "SEO IS DEAD" FALLACY

I cannot count the number of times I have heard "SEO is dead" at a marketing conference or read the statement in a publication. I even heard SEO would be dead by 2020 at the biggest SEO conference in the world by the keynote speaker (it is currently 2022, and SEO is nowhere near dead—the opposite actually). With each Google update comes a fresh batch of fear that the search engine will make webmasters irrelevant and brands will have to pay for their traffic.

It is all part of a larger worry or (in some cases) hopeful-
ness SEO is actually dead or dying. These theories leave
out who is being excluded and who is benefiting from the
updates (we know publishers and review sites are being
left behind while brands are benefiting). This gives leeway
to the idea of SEO "dying," but adds stipulations to the
concept. In a way, the "SEO is dead" fallacy has merit, but
in all the wrong ways. Let us explore and expand on this
concept.

First, here is a brief rundown of some changes that have
recently been made. These have impacted the changing
SEO landscape. Google made its SERP feature update a
few years back to give quick answers at the top of its search
engine result pages for all sorts of queries ranging from
"What is the temperature in Dallas?" to "How much do new
Slack users cost?" Quick answers are provided for these at
the top of the SERPs. Links are provided to the source of the
answer if it does not come from Google directly.

This cut out many websites. The biggest losers were
websites that dished out quick answers. This included
weather and conversion websites. Google went further and
made them their own product, placing those results at the
top as the truth. There was no need to continue on to a site
after getting an answer. For example, if you search for a time
zone conversion, Google will feed your answer in the SERP.
If you want to know the time in France, and Google gives

it to you right in the SERP, would you click into a few sites to verify? Unlikely. Your activity starts and ends on Google.

After this update, many tech publishers heralded the "end of SEO." They had the stance that Google's taking all the traffic now, so you should avoid getting into SEO. Although this can be discouraging, it does not have to be, and we can accept concerns and negative trends without giving up.

When I speak about SEO at marketing conferences, someone always asks me whether SEO is now dead because Google takes up more of the space in the SERPs. Many SERP features—especially those that provide answers to more complex questions—get a lot of clicks even though Google provides the user with an answer. In fact, many sites that conformed to Google's structure saw an increase in traffic from the change. Which websites got the most? Brands. How did this happen? Brands building domain authority wrote about more complex subjects.

This complexity leads to further curiosity for the Google user. That curiosity leads to the domain. This was an unintended consequence of Google's update to include SERP features. Brands got another leg up—more traffic, more backlinks, and better domain authority.

So, yes it is true SEO is getting less reliable if you are a website that provides up-to-date weather information, movie showtimes, definitions, or currency exchanges. But it is trending the opposite way for brands selling products or services. Quick answers to questions mean more searches from curious Google users. This further enhances Brand Primacy efforts.

THE "LITTLE THINGS DO NOT MATTER" FALLACY

All too often, those attempting to understand the world of SEO fall into the trap of believing the little things do not matter, when in fact they do. This is driven by numerous defeats at the hands of large domains, which leads people to believe there is nothing they can do to overtake the "big guys." It also gives the false idea a large domain does not need to adhere to the small details.

However, when it comes to SEO, the little things are actually big things, and you can use the competition's misunderstandings to your advantage by caring for the "small" details. By small, I mean things like no alt text on a photo, an article that does not pull in readers, a blog post without a catchy title, a meta description that does not intrigue, etc.

We can break this concept down into two piles: bigger picture SEO tasks and smaller picture SEO tasks. Things like technical SEO, content, URLs, and keyword maps fall into your "bigger picture" pile. The "smaller picture" tasks deal with images, link best practices, republishing, and article layout.

However, do not forget adhering to the bigger picture items is crucial, and no amount of tweaking the tiny tasks will give you a leg up on the competition if that is not top-notch in the first place. Once you feel comfortable with your major items, it is time to use SEO strategies that are lesser-known and often overlooked.

The reason this is so powerful is it is counterintuitive, since it is a common misconception that doing the small things does not have a big impact. By pushing back against this fallacy, you create leverage.

Take images, for example. We use them to break up text within articles, but they require specific attention to be seen as favorable in Google, and thus, not receive ranking disadvantages. It is common sense to use images that tie in nicely with the content, but there is more to it. SEO requires images to have strong, descriptive alt text and on-topic image text as well. Not only that, but the image's file name should share keywords with the article's main keyword. So for example, let us say you wrote an article targeting the keyword "software-bugs." If the link to the article was *www.(yoursite).com/blog/software-bugs*, you would want the images within the article to be named software-bugs-1, software-bugs-2, etc. Now let us say one of these images was a picture of a broken computer. The alt text should describe the image as if to someone visually impaired (since alt text is used for the visually impaired!). It might read "A picture of a desktop computer with a broken screen." The descriptive text underneath should reiterate the points made in the text corresponding to the picture.

Yes, these are smaller picture items, but neglecting them in favor of other SEO factors will cost you valuable spots in the rankings.

THE "SOMETIMES SLOPPY IS FINE" FALLACY

The "sometimes sloppy is fine" fallacy overlaps with the "it used to work so it always will" fallacy, and the "we are too big to fail" fallacy. Fortunately, those suffering from sloppy SEO are usually working with such large domains that being sloppy with SEO techniques is not that harmful.

However, as we have seen with Google and their continuous improvements to the algorithm, cutting corners and offering a substandard user experience is bound to catch up to even the biggest of domains. If you do not think it is a big deal, do a search for comments about the latest Google update (or any Google update for that matter). You will find many website owners are frustrated by the loss of rankings and traffic. This does not mean they did something wrong, but it shows changes are happening and they affect domains.

There is a common misconception that once an article is published and ranking well on Google, the work is done. Well, guess what? It is not. Far from it, in fact. Even your best articles that are ranked in the first slot (rank zero) need attention now and again. What kind of attention does this entail? It depends. Consider the changes Google adapts to their algorithm. Decide if there are adjustments that would improve your content. Continually strive to meet what Google wants: to deliver the best results to their users.

So, why exactly do we need to switch things up when we are first? Well, as you know, Google changes its algorithm all the time. What worked yesterday will not work today. On top of this, your competition is hungry, and you have got a target on your back. They want that rank zero spot, and they will do everything they can to copy and improve on your work. Remember in high school when a classmate got busted for plagiarizing? Well, there is no "teacher" on the internet to hold anyone accountable. The way you write an article—and definitely the ideas in it—will be copied. I once noticed four or five articles at the top of the SERP had all copied each other—and they all were wrong! The first article had made an error, and everyone else followed suit.

Here are some unique solutions to combat these fallacies. First, change your way of thinking so you are constantly fighting for quality.

For example, when it comes to your well-off articles, consider republishing them from time to time to stay current. Think about things like title changes, maybe include new topical ideas or putt a new year in the title. Also think about whether your images are working. And consider the structure of the article. Whatever it is, be sure it gives you a fighting chance to stay on top.

SOME THOUGHTS ABOUT PERFECTION

The final SEO advice is: the most common perfection philosophies are harmful to brands. I am going to put this in bold for emphasis, because it is one of the most important things you can ever learn about SEO: **this game, in which we are playing, is a race against time.** You are fighting both your industry competitors as well as the clock. Let us go into this further with an example I see companies fall victim to repeatedly.

Fictional company "Blue" is a SaaS (software as a service) company that sells business-based communication tools. They have researched and found there are six other brands directly competing with them in the same industry. They are behind their direct competition in sales and decide that to catch up with them, one of the things they want to focus on is SEO. They begin creating content for their blog, which has a chance to rank in Google and bring them new leads. After a bit of research, they find the most valuable keyword to bring in new clients is "business communication systems." Currently, they are ranking twelfth for this term. Their competitors are in the top six spots. They decide to republish their article, giving it a complete makeover. However, they are still working on the republish a few months later. They have been making small adjustments here and there to try to create the perfect article, one that will surely outrank the competition.

Do you see why Blue's decision to create a perfect piece of content might hurt them? If we consider they are trying to beat their competitors *and* the clock, they have already lost. Let me explain further. Let us say there are five thousand businesses looking for a business-based communication system each year. If, say, 95 percent of them have already committed to buying from Blue's competitors, what is left? Even if they create a majestic article that ranks first in Google, they can only scoop up the last 250 businesses. Again, this is a race against time. Get more of your content out there, ignore the perfectionists, and get yourself in the game. You will have plenty of time to make adjustments post-publish; winning on more search terms is key.

15

HOW DOES GOOGLE BENEFIT?

BEFORE I TALK ABOUT HOW GOOGLE BENEFITS FROM Brand Primacy, it is important to recap how companies can benefit. We will use "insurance" as an example. Insurance is one of the toughest keywords to rank for, with loads of monthly volume in the US. Though there is no exact amount, there are rough estimates the CPC, or cost per click, for the term "insurance" is nineteen dollars. When you consider this keyword is getting millions of clicks each month, you can see how valuable Brand Primacy is for companies. Ranking first in Google for "insurance" compared to ranking second is an astronomical difference in traffic.

By incentivizing brands to compete on Google with high-quality content, Google increasingly provides better and better content for searchers on their SERPs. Does this answer the question of how does Google benefit? Yes and no. On the one hand, we see Google receives high-quality content because they incentivize brands to create it. That is a direct benefit, but it is very simple and surface level. How does Google go about turning this into something they benefit from en masse?

For that, we have to talk about the dynamics of how Google allows advertisers to operate on its site. Not included in the book so far, though relevant here, is Google Ads or the paid advertisements above the organic rankings we have been discussing.

Instead of allowing advertisers to make whatever decisions they wanted, they encouraged quality ads through different standards—standards that ensure the Google customer receives quality ads. Google is doing the same thing for the organic search results. Want to get to the top? Give the user the best possible experience. No shortcuts.

Consider a workplace where all the employees hate their boss. It is safe to assume they will not give their best effort. Now, think of a workplace where the employees love their boss. Even if they are feeling a bit lazy, they will push through, knowing how important it is for their boss to see them succeed.

This scenario applies to Google's ranking system. Google wanted great content, the kind of stuff that could pull in hundreds of thousands of readers, no matter the topic. But, to do that, they would have to get people to write great content for Google's sake.

To accomplish this, they had to be the "nice boss," rewarding good content with good rankings. The brands build their domain authority, and Google obtains a lot of traffic from users searching for this great content. This naturally builds a great relationship between brands and Google—brands get more and cheaper sales from organic results in Google and Google gets great content for their users.

If everyone in the world wanted each article they read to have something about bananas in it, Google could incentivize brands to include bananas in each article. This would then bring everyone looking for bananas to Google because they would be the ones with all the banana content. Google did just that but with every industry.

Lastly, consider this example: someone does a Google search for train tracks, and the top result is an article by *USA Today*. The user clicks into it and realizes it requires a paywall (payment to read the article).

Though the search intent was technically answered correctly, the user experience sucked (since it is not fun to read an article with a giant blocker on it). By incentivizing brands to build their content up and be as strong as, say, articles by *USA Today*, Google solves the search intent while giving a great user experience. Brands selling products need the traffic to build domain authority, and they do not have a paywall. User experience feeds back into Google and the brand wins.

As you know from the chapter about SEO changes, that is Google's main concern—the user experience. As a result, brands have adapted—at least those who understand Brand Primacy. These fortunate ones are reaping the rewards of great exposure that previously would have gone to the paywall publishers of older times.

Tying everything together here, brands are building domain authority so Google can place them in front of customers. They do this by solving search intent and giving a strong user experience.

16

THOUGHTS ON A CHANGING SEARCH LANDSCAPE

SIGNIFICANT CHANGES RARELY HAPPEN OVERNIGHT. When we think of innovation, we picture immediate impact. Unfortunately, history shows us the process of replacing the old and implementing the new always lags. Entertainment provides an excellent example of this.

For thousands of years, people have been putting on plays. Actors and actresses graced the stage to perform for an audience, delivering stories in the form of live-action sequences that bring imagination to life. In the past century, plays evolved in style, presentation, technology/special effects, and more. This evolution, however, followed a pattern—the basis of the play, as a form, did not change. And as far as humans were concerned, if you wanted a story, you would either read one or hear someone tell one. If you wanted to *see* a story acted out, you watched a play. Then along came video cameras.

The magic of movies and film made everyone realize we no longer needed to put on plays to act out stories, right? Here we experience something hard to deny: the wheels of change turn slowly. When it came to the introduction of movies and video cameras, the big thinkers came up with this solution: put on a play and film it. Yes, that is correct: when they were first introduced, most movies were live plays with a camera rolling.

Are you familiar with the movie *The Wizard of Oz*? The film you are probably aware of is the 1939 version starring Judy Garland. However, most people do not realize there were other renditions of the popular book, one released in 1910, the other in 1925. These three movies provide an excellent demonstration of the slowly turning wheels of change in motion. Let us begin with the 1910 version.

Instead of moving from scene to scene with a general focus on a character and their story, the 1910 version moves along like a play, appearing as if the camera could only conceivably take the angle of an audience member before a stage in an auditorium. There are no shots behind, above, or to the side of the cast. The point of view is completely that of a person sitting in a seat in front of a stage. As we know now, this is a very limited scope of what movies can offer us.

Fifteen years from the initial 1910 release, another attempt was made with the 1925 film. Like the 1910 version, it is as if the camera was filming from a seat inside a theater auditorium. However, the difference is the film focuses on specific characters, particularly by zooming in on them. Imagine that—fifteen years down the line, and one of the only differences is the idea to focus on a specific cast member.

Finally, we move to the version most everyone is familiar with—the 1939 Judy Garland classic. Note the massive differences in how this film is shot compared to the earlier versions. Not in the technological advances, but in the strategic ways the movie was filmed, going away from the idea that a movie needs to be a play. The camera follows characters, it cuts away to different speakers and actions, it takes many different angles, etc. So, as we see, from 1910 to 1939, people figured out this new technology. It took twenty-nine years to understand a video camera could make movies instead of filmed versions of plays.

These "visionaries" did not understand how to separate themselves from the way they had always done things (in this case, use plays to act out stories), although they were amazed by the potential of new technology.

The bottom line is: no matter how different or unique new mediums are, they mostly follow the format of the old mediums.

THE NEW SERP

I do not have a crystal ball, but neither does anyone else. It is fair to say not even the engineers and developers at Google know what will happen in the future in terms of Brand Primacy. Reckless speculation can be harmful, but preparation based on calculated estimations is important.

The following ideas are what I feel will be most impactful and important to follow in the coming years of Brand Primacy. These will ultimately give you helpful ideas in your own campaign successes. Let us begin with the SERP and the changes it will face.

SERPs in the early 2010s went from explaining things with one or two relevant results, to very helpful articles explaining the same thing in uniform ways. SERPs are now becoming more and more like a magazine publication with a table of contents rather than a series of results explaining the same thing. In a search for a topic, you will find unique takes on a subject with catchy titles.

In fact, Brand Primacy demands this to be the case. The competitive nature of brands and their attempts to win in Google has affected the rankings and ensures a SERP will be diverse and filled with varying content. Results conveying the exact same message had no chance once brands realized they had the power to be first in so many generic search term rankings. Just like a magazine, the SERPs now deliver different genres on the first page.

The content inside of those search results is also changing dramatically. In the past, you would find articles that were not comprehensive or were unhelpful listicles. Now, you find highly authoritative and comprehensive articles (written mainly by brands that sell products) that break down the topic at hand without selling users something. In the future, then, it makes sense to assume the types of articles best fitting into the SERP will be ones free of salesy language.

These articles also have excellent graphics—videos and are fully developed to be readable. Users now find these results accessible and better reads than previous ones throughout history. This led to brands becoming the modern publishers.

BRANDS WILL BEGIN TO BE PUBLISHERS

I love to read the Ahrefs blog for its rich, featured content around specific topic areas. As an SEO solution, their articles skew toward a search audience, but I visit them to get insightful information around technical topics because they do it the best. What has driven them to produce this excellent content? Arguably, Google.

Since they have a steady audience from Google and aspire to Brand Primacy, they publish these articles in their field. The SERP competition has given them an incentive to build better content to beat their competitors. The result is the best content in the industry.

But what is the next step? Since they have all this traffic, companies will begin to build more content for a returning audience. Most of that content will be topical pieces on new things going on in their market.

So eventually, brands will become news organizations. You could make the argument that many, like HubSpot, already have. They are even separating their domain and blog with different navigation, appearance, and feel.

They have editors, heads of content, and publishing schedules. They need to take one more step to become publishers: give editorial freedom to their content team. Do not bind them to their product, but treat them as an online newspaper with one sponsor: the brand. They should do this so they can continue building the brand and increasing traffic to the domain.

If a normal publisher was given the same advantages as a brand, they could do evergreen content and have a steady flow of traffic for regular readers. That is currently what brands have at their disposal.

Not all newspapers have banner ads or are behind paywalls. And the material might be higher quality, especially when it comes to fact checking. However, what Google wants matters. And Google does not care as much about these issues.

But brands have another advantage: they do not need to monetize with banner ads or subscriptions. The value they get from Brand Primacy alone is worth the effort. Banner ads are annoying and slow down websites. And nobody likes to pay for content.

MONETIZING WILL CHANGE: THE PERSPECTIVE OF PUBLISHERS

Anyone familiar with Google's initial ventures into monetizing their products understands how drastically different the process became over time. Even products and systems that lack major changes undergo a monetization change.

Conversely, this type of change is prevalent within a conversation about Brand Primacy and its future impacts.

Let us begin by talking about publishers and their monetization challenges. Making money as a publisher is difficult, even for the biggest publications out there. For example, I recently bought a subscription to *The Wall Street Journal (WSJ)* online. At around twenty-five dollars a month (once it passes its trial period), it is double the cost of a Netflix or Amazon Prime subscription. So, I was surprised to see *The WSJ* still places banner ads within their content. They are stuck between a rock and a hard place. On the one hand, they have to bring in enough money to stay afloat. However, the subscriptions are not bringing enough in. They could attempt to get more subscriptions, which I am sure they do, but are not as successful as they would like.

They could forgo the banner ads in favor of a higher subscription price, which might deter customers. And let me point out this is *The Wall Street Journal*, a highly respected, popular publisher. Not even the subscription model saves publications; they are still forced to monetize with annoying banner ads.

Here is where it gets interesting and shines serious light on Brand Primacy. Brands such as HubSpot do not need to do either of these things (subscription model or banner ads). They monetize their blog solely with Brand Primacy and its benefits to sales of their software.

The worlds of publishing and brands are beginning to collide, and in the coming years they will clash even more. In the example above, we see how differently monetization is for brands selling products compared to publishers. We have already looked at this through the lens of the brand, but how about the publisher? Since they have to monetize through insufficient subscriptions and banner ads, they will have a stake in brands.

Their massive domains will be leveraged to create Brand Primacy for their brands and these companies' user bases will be built on the data of *The Washington Post* or *The New York Times*. Essentially, publishers have pieces of a potentially successful Brand Primacy process. They could offer up these pieces to a brand that uses them more efficiently—an equally satisfying result for both parties. As for the individual user, they are the ultimate beneficiary when performing a Google search. What this means, essentially, is the large brands/publishers falling behind will offer up their positions to the highest bidder.

We need to consider how they can support Brand Primacy for multiple domains. The answer lies in the same way

HubSpot separates its blog from the shop for its product: subdomains. Imagine hubspot.nytimes.com or marketo. washingtonpost.com. This is the direction we are trending in the time of Brand Primacy.

Brands built upon subdomains will have a degree of separation from the publications both with the user and with Google. This allows Brand Primacy to flourish for the companies. And gone will be the days of crazy spellings to secure a cheap domain. Brands using a subdomain of an existing massive domain can use any name they choose.

The Washington Post is already doing this to some degree. Amazon could as well if they make it a part of their Amazon Prime membership. The publication serves as a draw to Amazon Prime, which is a Trojan horse to complete dominance of e-commerce.

When publishers co-opt a brand, they reap the rewards of their domain. Domain authority, especially for B2B SaaS companies, is massively profitable. They will not need subscribers or even banner ads; their products will pay the bills. They (publishers) can then offer up content that no longer requires banner ads or a paywall. And the brands will benefit from low-cost sales and brand awareness.

THE ADVENT OF THE CONTENT MARKETER JOURNALIST

Content manager, copywriter, content specialist—all these titles have popped up in digital marketing since the beginning of the drive toward Brand Primacy. On LinkedIn alone there are around five million people globally with the title of content manager.

But nobody would ever mistake these folks for journalists. They are marketers, even though many perform the same function as a journalist for a digital publication. Conversely, digital publication editors are beginning to function more like content managers. Advertorials pay the bills, and reviewing a product a company has paid you to review brings the advertorial lens to the piece.

These two positions are on a path of convergence, with more editors becoming content managers, and vice versa. What will protect journalistic integrity for digital publications is not the subscription model, but the monetization we discussed in the last section.

With companies hiring content managers to perform their duties with journalistic integrity, these publications will herald the advent of the content marketer journalist. No more will the job title be associated with marketing. The performance of these jobs will be editorial.

Companies will give freedom to their heads of content to provide the best information on a certain topic so long as it aligns with the topic area of their service and builds Brand Primacy. The shift from editors at digital publications will be simple, as many of them already complain about sales putting too many advertorials on their editorial calendar.

These will no longer be a factor as building Brand Primacy is an end in and of itself. There is no need for a hard sell when building Brand Primacy.

PUBLISHERS QUIT PLAYING GOOGLE'S GAME

Major publications like *The New York Times* and *The Washington Post* have shifted on their Google policy in the last few years. Before, these publications were indexed and you could search to find an entire article.

Eventually, a paywall would hit you after enough visits. Now, these are indexed, but do not show the reader everything on the page. Most make you log in or pay to read them. But this relationship cannot continue. We have already seen Google end indexing on LinkedIn because so much of the information is behind a login screen. Google wants the information it serves its users to be open for all to view. Paywalls are the opposite of this.

One of two things is eventually going to happen. Either Google stops indexing publications without open information, or publications begin to shift their monetization strategy. If Google stops indexing publishers and stops serving them on all of their results, including Google News and Discover, then publishers will take a large enough hit to make them reconsider their monetization policy.

The same result will happen with either scenario. The only other option is for these publications to cede their authority to up-and-coming brand publications.

A SHIFT FROM UNIVERSITIES TO BRANDS

As you have now seen in the above examples, brands are siphoning things like credibility and trust away from universities. There are further ideas in this category to consider. One way that highlights this concept is the shift in how certain projects are undertaken or seen by the public.

One way to illuminate this idea is the concept of a lecture. Years ago, this would have prompted us to think of a professor standing at the front of an auditorium on a university campus, delivering a roughly one-hour speech to a live audience.

They would repeat this throughout the day to different groups, delivering the same speech repeatedly.

Brand Primacy has made this into a completely different reality. First, as has been mentioned already, the content is different. Brands are now the ones creating lectures, and these are the ones Google is serving its users.

Thus, the lecture content the average person will see on a topic will be created by brands. Second, the way the lecture is delivered has changed as well. Brands thrive through creative efficiency, which means they have adapted the way they provide lectures.

They no longer require a live setting, but instead record a lecture and put it online for all to watch. No one is forced to give the same speech over and over, since it is done after one try. This also frees up any potential time restrictions since users can see the lecture regardless of the time of day.

So, we can start to make reasonable assumptions that based on these shifts, Brand Primacy can and will change the way we do things in the future. The lectures are one example of something already affected.

Another important example is in how brands are taking up the space that universities used to hold digitally in respect to articles. Now, content found on Google (often created by brands) is making its way into universities. The university has become too slow at creating articles that are delivered instantaneously without numerous processes on things like social media.

At first glance, this might seem like a scary prospect—the idea universities will be replaced and their expertise disregarded on Google searches. However, it can and should be seen as liberating. In a way, information from universities has been shackled and repressed from the general public. Though there is a watering-down effect of the quality of information, the trade-off is brands are working hard to deliver the goods to all people.

Similarly, there will come different ways for the average user to learn new things.

To see this shift in action and see why it is happening, pull up Google Scholar and try a few searches for business-relevant topics. You will notice lackluster results. Next, compare the same search with a normal Google search. You will find more helpful results because brands are willing to put out better information to gain traffic.

CHANGES IN HOW WE CONSUME INFORMATION

As brands become more trusted, we will begin to treat them as the top sources available. This is a slow process that is both inevitable and already happening. No one will wake up one day and notice brands are the ones giving us our information.

Likely, most people already consume most of their information using the data Google feeds them, which is mostly brands. Of course, they realize they are not looking at an academic journal, but they have become accustomed to taking what they are given in search results at face value. What has already started to happen will eventually solidify and become an unrecognizable norm, where Brand Primacy has resulted in a total change in the information we consume and how we do so.

There are still a few stragglers, and plenty of searches still go unsatisfied by the SERPs in the age of Brand Primacy. However, eventually the final holdouts will adjust to taking brands as truth and search for things written by brands rather than authors and major publications.

Even if the information is not up to standard, the process of deep-diving through endless search engine results is tedious. And finally, even in the situations where it makes sense to take extra time to locate more relevant information, these situations will change so users prefer the brand content no matter the search.

So, what are some ways this could change not only what the users are fed, but the information they desire? Consider how searchers are satisfied by the results brands offer. People searching for a wide variety of things find them at an extremely high rate on Google.

This proves Google is not pulling the wool over the user's eyes. Instead, the user is accepting the new reality of brands and prefers the type of content they are being delivered, as they are returning to it time and time again.

Lastly, when considering the "how"—as in, how we consume information—it will change to meet the new realities of what is available, what is convenient, and what is trusted. If it is convenient to find, for example, information on the first page rather than thirty-second, it will be selected further. And finally, if Google trusts it, the consumer will trust it as well. Others who do not trust Google may use different search engines, but the same principles will also apply there.

Now, let us jump from this point about consuming information into a relevant topic, which is how Google will change.

GOOGLE WILL CHANGE

This is not speculation as much as it is an ongoing reality: Google will permanently alter the way we consume information, but at the same time will change the way SERPs look.

When we consider the way Google shifts learning landscapes, it shows the power brands hold, as they are responsible for providing the best information in a convenient way and up to Google's standards.

Google is the same way. Everyone currently uses it the same way they use a textbook. However, the SERPs, or textbook layout, will change in the future, disrupting and changing the way people consume information.

Even though the results may stay the same, with Brand Primacy the changes in layout will alter which things users access. This is something brands are adapting to, but they need to remain vigilant for the potential future changes.

How it impacts brands directly, apart from their role in feeding content to users on Google, is in their potential outreach from search. If two competing brands share the first page SERP at the rank zero and first spots, it is safe to say a wide portion of users who search their keywords will visit both brand sites—the rank zero will get more visits, but both will get visits.

However, take that same example of competing brands and adapt the search to a mobile result in which the SERP only feeds the top brand, and you have a largely different industry with a completely new base of customers and customer knowledge.

This is more than speculation. Adaptation will be necessary the same way it was necessary when Google came to power. Other search engines were not as focused on delivering great results and user experience, which is one of the reasons Google charged ahead.

A similar thing could happen in the future, and Google will be at a crossroads. It is fair to say Google might choose better and undertake the necessary changes to please the user. However, it is also possible their vision falls short, and another way to search emerges. Whichever the case, the brands that will benefit from this most are the ones willing to seek out ideas like Brand Primacy and mold themselves accordingly.

EPILOGUE

THE MISTAKES OF HISTORY ON REPEAT

THERE IS AN IRONY LURKING HERE, WHICH IS CONNECTED to both Brand Primacy and Google. It overlaps between both stories and is a great way to close this book. As anyone who has researched Google knows, its history is filled with new ideas, ideas that challenge the status quo, ideas that are hard to grasp.

These new ideas and fresh perspectives then go through a very binary process. Either somebody says yes to the new way of thinking and embraces it, or they fall by the wayside by saying no. At some point, everyone realized the Google way was the way of the future, but not everyone fully committed.

These are the ones who failed, and probably do not even exist anymore. And, if they do exist, it is secondary to Google (think Yahoo!). The irony, then, as this relates to Brand Primacy, is it undergoes a similar process. Some brands embraced Google as truth and adapted to the reality of Brand Primacy, and others fell behind.

We now see this in the way brands go about building blogs and writing articles. They have a binary decision to make as well. Do we embrace Brand Primacy or not? Those that do, succeed within the system of Google, which as you know by now, is the system we live in. Those who do not, fail. It really is that simple, as if it were the difference between a "yes" or "no."

Another irony you might have already picked up on is the way Google, as a company, initially handled search results versus what types of talent reign supreme on those same search results. Although, the word "irony" only scratches the surface of this contrast in styles. Read any published work concerning Google's meteoric rise and you will notice one common denominator—those involved were focused on mathematics, systems, and accurately calibrated scientific schemes designed to make their search deliver strong results.

That is not to say they were not creative when they needed to be, but there was a methodical banality. The irony, then, comes from how different their search results handle rankings now. A brand that wants to be at the top can get there through a creative approach, free of mathematical systems.

As we move in whichever direction the world of SEO and search engines takes us, awareness is the main thing to note. Being aware of what is working and valuable in the moment is what matters most. For you, Brand Primacy is now at the forefront of your mind, and that is good, because it is the big thing right now. It is the current moment, and all that is needed is for good brands to jump in and make a difference for themselves and their potential customers.

Of course, it is easy to look at past mistakes and proclaim we will steer clear of them. However, when the subject in the future is filled with uncertainties, clarity comes in the actions you take rather than those you avoid. Brand Primacy has taken center stage as the solution to past mistakes, and brands have aligned themselves accordingly.

The only thing left to do is join them, because it makes all the sense in the world to go after what you deserve and what you are destined to achieve. Google is waiting. If the mistakes of history are repeating, they stop here.

ABOUT THE AUTHOR

CORY SCHMIDT IS A LEADING EXPERT IN THE SEO FIELD, having taken many companies to the Google search rankings promised land. He has been a speaker at many marketing, sales, web development, and SEO seminars. He is a marketing and sales leader at tech companies. When he is not finding innovative ways to disrupt the world of marketing, he likes to travel, read, and write.